How to Talk with Sick, Dying, and Grieving People

How to Talk with Sick, Dying, and Grieving People

When There are No Magic Words

Patrick Riecke

Emerald Hope Publishing House

Fort Wayne

Copyright © 2018 by Patrick S. Riecke

All rights reserved. This book or any portion thereof may not be reproduced or used in any manner whatsoever without the express written permission of the publisher except for the use of brief quotations in a book review.

Scripture taken from the Holy Bible, NEW INTERNATIONAL VERSION ®, NIV ®, Copyright © 1973, 1978, 1984, 2011 by Biblica, Inc.® Used by permission. All rights reserved worldwide.

NEW INTERNATIONAL VERSION® and NIV® are registered trademarks of Biblica, Inc. Use of either trademark for the offering of goods or services requires the prior written consent of Biblica US, Inc.

Dedication

I dedicate this book to my children. Daniel, Aidan, Levi, and Kelsey, you have kept my life interesting. None of you tolerate anything disingenuous. For that I am grateful. You are four of the most sincere people on the face of the planet. As you know, my prayer is that you are the person you are supposed to be. No one else can be you—so you had better do it.

I love you.

Contents

Endorsements	xi
Foreword	xiii
Preface: No Magic Words	1
1 Unprepared for Life (And Death)	7
2 Spiritual Life: Phase One and Phase Two	20
3 Lessons from Job	30
4 How to Visit the Hospital	52
5 Phase Three and The Moment of Death	68
6 The Role of Faith Leaders	78
7 5 Mistakes to Avoid in Phase Three	85
8 Waiting for a Miracle, Playing God, and Advance Care Planning	98
9 Faith Vs. Medicine: Dignify the Dying Person	119

10	How to Talk with a Grieving Person	*133*
11	Finding Meaning in Suffering	*149*
12	No Matter How Small: Understanding Miscarriage and Stillbrith	*170*

Help-Sheet #1: Healthcare Terms	*181*
Help-Sheet #2: HIPAA and Privacy	*185*
Help-Sheet #3: Patient Rights	*187*
Help-Sheet #4: Medical Ethics FAQs	*189*
Help-Sheet #5: Tips for Hospital Visitation	*193*
Acknowledgements	*199*
More Grief Resources	*202*

Endorsements

"Go, sit down, shut up and cry," (page 44). If that is all one takes from this book, it would be worth it, but there is so much more! Patrick shares, with refreshing authenticity, from his personal life as well as his professional experience. Patrick's kind heart can be felt as one reads his words; he is a perfect example of the presence we should bring to each person. Patrick offers specific, simple, and practical advice for being with the sick, dying, and grieving and generally everybody. "Go, sit down, shut up and cry" is exactly what I hope someone would do for me. Thanks, Patrick.

Jane Munk, Founder of *Kerith Brook*, Retreats for Grieving Adults

This book should be used as a guide for all when we are called to support people who are ill, people who are facing death, and bereaved people. Many of us struggle with what to say, and sometimes, while trying to be supportive, we can say something that is not helpful, even hurtful. The author offers practical tips about walking alongside those who are suffering. He also eloquently uses one man's personal story to highlight the value of talking about and documenting wishes and choices about future medical care. The identification of the Three Phases of Spiritual Growth and the stories shared affirmed my belief that we can all find more effective ways to comfort others experiencing life-altering situations.

Chris Brinneman, MSW, LCSW, Manager of Advance Care Planning

Foreword

No Magic Words indeed!

I have never thought of myself as a sensitive person. Few others have, either. I'm a wise-cracker who prefers to keep his own feelings hidden and prefers not to think about others' feelings.

The problem is, I do have feelings, pretty deep ones sometimes. And as a self-described Christ-follower, I'm supposed to acknowledge, even care for, others' feelings.

So I don't do well with recognizing and expressing my feelings or with responding to others' feelings. I'd sooner avoid them. But I can't. I dare not.

That's why I need the insights in this book.

Like the author, I'm trained for ministry. In fact, most of my career has been training people for ministry. Patrick Riecke happens to be one of those people.

People in ministry (that is, people who serve others in the name of Jesus, not just professional clergy) get to be present with others in crisis. Notice I say "get to," not just "have to." What starts as an obligation is discovered to be a blessing when it's carried out.

We who aspire to serve and who undertake the training generally expect to be told "the right thing to say" in every possible situation. We are fond of looking back and saying, "No one taught me how to handle this," as if it's an indictment of our teachers. We're supposed to be the answers-people.

But the reality is that the true God does the greatest work through weak vessels, through people who don't know any "magic words," who realize that their answers aren't what is needed in the moment of pain. God can do this greatest work through those who seem naturally sympathetic, who in their sensitivity would never think of themselves as strong. But that work can also be done through knuckleheads like me, who like to act strong and give sharp answers to cover for our weaknesses.

Foreword

This book is all about embracing the weakness, the inability any of us have to figure out the right thing to say or to do. It tells us that our presence and our true feelings are the balms that through us God gives to those who are fearful as death approaches and grieving as death has come. Its author is a real pro, a supervisor of hospital chaplains who daily comfort people impacted by the scourge of death. But this book is not technical. It is true and elegant in its simplicity. It tells us that we can all do this, with the stuff we were made with if we take the pressure off ourselves to be smart and strong. It shows us how to walk by faith through the valley of death.

Along the way, this book will also share some related useful advice about preparing for a future medical crisis with Advanced Directives. As I read it, I resolved to update my paperwork, for the sake of those I love.

But mostly, I resolved to be present for those in pain, to sit down, be quiet, shed the tears that come naturally, and learn with those who suffer the things that God teaches us only in suffering.

The true God knows all about our suffering. In Jesus, God the Son became one of us, suffering and dying as we all do. In that climax of all this work, God experienced the same grief that we experience when our loved ones die. For our sakes, God became weak. Perhaps that is why God teaches us and uses us in our weakest moments.

But that is an answer. I need to be quiet with those who suffer.

Jon Weatherly, PhD
Professor of New Testament
Vice President for Academic Affairs/Provost
Johnson University

Preface: No Magic Words

You will encounter powerful, moving stories in this book. I had tears in my eyes while writing or remembering many of them. They have a common thread: at least one character in each story was overwhelmed with so much pain, trauma, fear, or grief that there were no magic words that could be said to make things better.

A man yells at God after his wife dies.

A young woman isn't sure if she will be able to overcome her cancer diagnosis.

A silver-haired man suffers a stroke and can no longer feed himself breakfast.

"We all want to hug you. Will that be okay?" The young man, whose mom had tragically and suddenly died that day, quietly nodded; so I wrapped my arms around him. "I'm so sorry. I wish there were some magic words I could say to make it all better."

In life's most difficult moments, we all want to help or to say the right thing, but it can feel like all the rules of life have suddenly changed.

I am Rev. Patrick Riecke, M.A., and I am the Director of Chaplains and Chairperson of the Ethics Committee for Parkview Health, Indiana, USA. Over the past twenty years, I have curated the best methods for helping people and families in exactly these moments. In this book, I will unveil:

- Compelling stories of ultimate suffering and significance
- Must-do actions for those who want to help
- Traps to avoid so you can be successful at making a difference
- Three case studies of hurting people and how to help
- Actions to *Always, Never, or Sometimes* take

when you visit a hospital
- My *Three Phases of Spiritual Growth*
- How to talk with a person in grief. What NOT to say, and what TO say instead.
- Practical tips for leaders who care about people in grief, trauma, or crisis

The skeleton of this book was developed for day-long workshops presented to groups, so sometimes the dialogue of these workshops has directly influenced the feel of the text. In other places, you will have the chance to dive deeper, because you are a reader of this text instead of a participant in a workshop.

Why did I write this book? Because hundreds of opportunities to help people in moments of physical, medical, and spiritual crises have shown me that those of us who want to help need a forum to collect our thoughts before we can be helpful to those who need us the most when they need us the most.

Who is this book for? Let me answer that with a very brief story.

One Saturday, my family and I were playing miniature golf when my phone rang. The voice on the other end was a friend of ours named Lori.

"My friend's baby just died."

Lori was in shock.

Should I go to the hospital? What should I say? Will the baby be in the room? Why would this have happened? How will she respond? Can she have a funeral?"

Lori cares about her friend very much.

And when this tragedy struck, she wanted to know how to help.

She knows there are no magic words.

I wrote this book for Lori and future Loris.

This book is for people who want to help in real ways and understand that hard times affect the mind, heart, and spirit in mysterious ways. These pages will allow you a behind-the-scenes look at making a real difference for people in real difficulties.

What follows is a pilgrimage into the world that we would all like to avoid, but none of us can.

Welcome to the unavoidable, sacred, and sometimes very meaningful world that words cannot describe.

I call it "Phase Three".

For more great content, subscribe to Patrick and Kristen Riecke on YouTube.

ch. 1

Unprepared for Life (And Death)

To hear me tell this story on YouTube, search Patrick and Kristen Riecke on YouTube and select the video entitled: "Introduction: How to Talk with Sick, Dying, and Grieving People"

My hospital day was Wednesday. I worked at a church with several clergy members on staff. We each took one day a week to visit our people in the hospital.

I did not look forward to these visits.

Not only was I primarily working with young people at the time, but I was also still young myself.

If I am honest, I looked at hospital visits as a hassle.

These were the days before many privacy laws, so we had a simple way to track our members who were sick or hospitalized. A large dry-erase board was located between my office and the next. Written in black, smelly markers were the names of area hospitals. Under each hospital name were the names of the people from the church who were in that hospital. Their room numbers, health concerns, and other information was scrawled in green, blue, and red smelly markers.

One Wednesday, I had put off my hospital visit as long as possible. Finally, out of obligation, I stepped out of my office and looked at the board, hoping there would be exactly zero names of people for me to visit. To my disappointment, there was one name written in blue marker. She was listed under Parkview Hospital, an urban hospital with a dated and snug parking garage, a long walk in, and a welcoming staff.

I hopped into my tan Buick with the dented front fender and headed the short drive down State Boulevard to see Gladys (not her real name—privacy expectations have increased since that time).

Searching for a parking spot, my wheels squeaked as I rounded each corner in the garage. I remembered what the whiteboard had told me about Gladys. It wasn't much.

It just said, "broken hip".

It seemed pretty typical to me. You know, "Old woman falls, breaks hip." And to me, broken hips belonged in the same category as broken arms or legs. In other words, I was thinking that a little bit of time at the hospital and Gladys would be good as new. A little speedbump to overcome, for sure.

But not life and death. Or was it?

Donning my "visiting minister" badge, I asked the volunteer at the front desk for directions to Gladys's room. The brick and tile infrastructure of the hospital was familiar to me. And my favorite part was welcoming smells wafting from the elaborate coffee cart in the lobby. I made plans to get a frozen something-or-other on my way out. Then I headed to the nearby elevators and punched the button for the third floor.

When I reached Gladys's room, she was alone.

I knocked. She didn't respond.

I slowly stepped in, my anxiety building. I didn't like doing this and my main goal was to get out as soon as possible. I was happy there was no family in the room because I wouldn't need to meet anyone new; and I could probably get out more quickly. It wasn't until I was alongside her bed that I could see her face.

Gladys was crying.

I did the only thing I knew how. I pulled a chair up close and sat down. I introduced myself because Gladys and I had never met before. I said what I often did in these situations, "Pastor Bob (our older, senior pastor) asked me to visit." She nodded in recognition of Bob's name, and in doing so seemed to accept me as a representative of her community—someone she could trust to care about her and her situation.

Her tears still flowed. She didn't say much, lying there in the typical hospital gown. I stepped out to ask the nurse if Gladys was ok. She explained that Gladys needed surgery, but it had been a bit delayed.

"She's just in a lot of pain. She broke her hip." The nurse looked at me like I didn't get it.

That's because I didn't get it.

My confused look faded as I sat back down next to Gladys's bed. I leaned forward and said the only thing I could come up with.

"How can I pray for you?" I asked the woman who was about six decades older than me.

"Sonny," she said, without seeming condescending, "Just pray for me to go be with Jesus."

Pray for her to go be with Jesus? You could have knocked me over with a feather. This woman "just" had a broken hip and she wanted… to *die*?

I began to understand that day that pain leads to problems.

Trauma leads to questions.

Disease can raise spiritual questions that pierce the heart.

And there are no magic words to say at a time like this.

UNPREPARED

A friend told me his story of when words failed. He had befriended a family who had experienced the tragic death of a teenage son. My friend has a wonderful heart. As such, he had cared for them, let them talk about their grief, had prayed for them, etc. Then, out of the blue, the father had a massive stroke.

Tests the next day confirmed everyone's greatest fear. This man, still young himself, was declared brain dead.

In the hospital waiting room, the man's wife, already broken with her son's death, turned to my friend and asked, "What do you think, should we donate his organs?"

What my friend said next as we ate our lunch of tacos in the dining room of the medical center where I work is something I have heard many times. "They didn't teach us how to handle these situations in school."

No kidding. I love the two institutions where I was educated as an adult. And while they prepared me in many ways, it's next to impossible to train anyone how to respond in the most difficult moments in life.

+++

In the humid days of August one year, the hospital experience became personal for me.

And, again, I was unprepared.[1]

---

1. To help you be more prepared for your next visit to the hospital, request your free Wallet Card via mail at PatrickRiecke.com/Resources

Unprepared

My oldest son, Daniel, had been sick with the stomach flu for more than a week. At the age of eleven, he laid on the couch all day, every day. If you have been around an 11-year-old boy, you know it is unusual for them to hold still very long. Also, he wasn't eating (also out of character for a young boy), and he had lost more than a pound per day during his illness.

We had taken Daniel to see the doctor the week before, but since he wasn't improving we scheduled another appointment.

My wife, Kristen, and I have four children. And they are all close in age. In fact, at that time Daniel was 11 years old, Aidan was 10, and Levi was 9. Kelsey, our princess, was in Kindergarten.

The real surprise while Daniel was sick? No one else had come down with the flu–yet. We went more than a week all cooped up in the same house without anyone else joining in the nausea and vomiting fun. Until day number eight.

In the middle of the night, Aidan woke up and suddenly got sick as kids do. He had a fever. Mom and dad were not surprised.

Since Daniel had an appointment the next day, we called and asked if we could just bring Aidan along. We wanted him to be seen as well. I'm pretty sure that doctors hate it when you do that.

But, they obliged.

We love Dr. Bollier. A few years older than my wife and me, he has served not only as a pediatrician but as a mentor. His bearded face, sports conversation, and faith focus were always welcome. He is thorough, but not alarmist. He takes his time. He listens. He's a pillar of our community, and we wouldn't trade him for anyone else.

That day he looked over Daniel first, who had lost eleven pounds—a lot for a young person.

"Well Daniel, I think you are going to be ok. Just hang in there. You're not dehydrated. It's just a bad case of the flu."

Dr. Bollier was his usual calm and reassuring presence.

Next up was little brother. Aidan stood to face Dr. Bollier. His eyes were red and he was on the verge of tears. He had gotten sick several times through the night and was spent.

After his reassuring words about Daniel, I fully expected a similar diagnosis for Aidan.

But Dr. Bollier started having Aidan do things he hadn't asked Daniel to do.

"Bend over and touch your toes, Aidan" Dr. Bollier instructed.

Aidan winced in pain as he tried to comply. I didn't think much of it. I haven't been able to touch my toes since I was an infant.

"Turn your head this way. Now the other way. Tilt it this way, now that way." Dr. Bollier guided.

"Ow," said Aidan, "I can't."

Aidan's tears broke through.

Dr. Bollier's pace and tone changed slightly as he turned and to face me.

Next came the question for which I was unprepared.

"Which hospital do you prefer?" Dr. Bollier was just a couple feet in front of me as he stared into my face for my answer, just a bit impatient.

"Well, I prefer to not go to the hospital at all," is what I was thinking. But I stammered out my answer.

"Um, well, Parkview I guess," I indicated the same hospital where I had visited Gladys years before, now in a new location.

His next words shook me to my core. He had never been didactic and demanding in the years I had known him. Until now.

"You're going to leave here right now and take Aidan to the Emergency Department at Parkview. When you leave, I will call the hospital and ask them to be ready for you. They will want to do a spinal tap on Aidan."

"I think he has meningitis."

Now my tears came near the surface.

Aidan was in full cry. Big brother, peaked from more than a week of the flu, looked like a bolt of lightning had just shot through him. Daniel is the most protective person I have ever met. He flew into command (and panic) mode. He pushed me and Aidan out the door and to our car. As they loaded into the back seat of our silver mini-van, Aidan's hands began to extend in such a way that he could not contract them.

"Daaaaad!" came the cry from his older brother.

I phoned Kristen. I tried to speak calmly so she would not panic.

I was unsuccessful.

We arrived at the hospital, and everything went into fast forward.

We watched Aidan, our fourth-grader, get an IV, blood draws, and a spinal tap. He was admitted to the pediatric unit. He was placed under precautions, which meant that everyone who came to see us had to wear a gown, gloves, and mask.

We were told that in twenty-four hours we would know if the meningitis was viral or bacterial. We learned that we wanted him to have viral meningitis because bacterial is the one that kills people.

That night I was on duty as a chaplain at the same hospital where my son was a patient. I confess I visited one patient more than others that during that shift.

A long twenty-four hours later we learned the good news—it was viral. Aidan was already feeling much better. Another twenty-four hours and he was discharged with no ill effects.

But in that short period, we were introduced to the full spectrum of emotions, fears, and spiritual questions that come up when faced with a serious illness, injury, or disease.

We felt very much unprepared, even though I was part of the care team at that very hospital.

Again, there were no magic words.

THE JOURNEY AHEAD

In the coming pages, we will take a deep dive into situations like these three stories. Situations where life turns upside down.

We will encounter the process of spiritual growth through pain and learn how someone like you can both understand it for yourself and help others who are facing their most difficult times.

We'll use case studies extensively, touch on ancient insights, grapple with letting go, death, and grief.

I'll give you practical hospital tips, and conversational tools you will use to help people as their world turns upside down.[2]

---

[2]. My video course provides 18 short videos on these topics that you can view on demand. PatrickRiecke.com/Courses

Spiritual Life: Phase One and Phase Two

ch. 2

BETHANY

Bethany has been a part of your place of worship since she was a child. Her dad is one of the leaders at church. You've known this family for a long time.

Although Bethany is a little younger than you, the two of you have been good friends for many years.

Bethany met Brad in college and they were married shortly after graduation. Now they have three children; Haley, a middle school daughter, Micah, a son in elementary school, and Emma is their baby girl.

Bethany

During Bethany's pregnancy with Emma, a regular ultrasound showed that the baby was fine. However, there was a concern for Bethany. After Emma was born, a screening was done that showed a mass on one of Bethany's ovaries. And after some more testing, your phone rang. It was Bethany's dad.

You could tell he had been crying. What he said next confirmed your fears.

"It's cancer." He said. "Ovarian cancer. Stage three, near stage four. We need to get everyone praying. We need a miracle."

PHASES OF SPIRITUAL GROWTH

We'll spend quite a bit of time with Bethany and her family, but let's ask ourselves a question before we go on.

Does your spiritual life today (your values, beliefs, whether religious or not) look like your spiritual life five years ago? Do you have the identical beliefs and values that you did five years ago?

What about twenty years ago?

Of course not. What has changed?

More importantly, why have you changed?

Most of us would have a common thread in our answers to that question.

I would point to a few reasons why I have changed. First, I would point to a miscarriage that my wife and I experienced.[1] Next, a couple of major disappointments in my ministry career. Then, to the births of my children. Finally, other losses, pains, and watching others go through hard times.

The bottom line is that pain and problems lead us to change in many ways.

What follows is an oversimplification, but it will help us as we think about pain and spiritual growth.

I will describe three phases of growth. These phases specifically relate to our experience of pain, loss, and disappointment.

PHASE ONE

The theme of Phase One of our spiritual journey is:

Phase One: God loves you and has a wonderful plan for your life.

---

1. For a word on the topic of baby loss, see the postscript of this book

Bethany

This is where the story of faith usually begins. In some Christian circles, we might call this the Gospel. It is good news we usually share with people as they enter the community of faith. It's conventional spiritual wisdom. The theme verse is often Jeremiah 29:11, "I know the plans I have for you, declares the Lord, plans to prosper you and not to harm you. Plans to give you hope and a future." *[out of context]*

Perhaps there was a time that you accepted a truth like this as you began your faith journey.

For me, I can clearly remember the April day in 1996 as I sat in a small church sanctuary, bulletin in hand. Having heard a sermon preached, I sang the worship song (badly).

My heart had been stirred for months, and that was the day I felt compelled to put my trust in this message that God cares about me, and that he wants to be involved in my life.

It certainly wasn't the first time I had been told this truth, but it was the first time I had heard it. That day I confessed faith and was baptized.

In my case, I felt that good news was compelling me to give my life to the ministry of some kind.

A few months later I entered Johnson Bible College, studying Bible and Preaching Ministry.

Although each of our stories is different, many people I have met have had some kind of experience like this as their faith journey began.

It is often serene and loving. We use words like 'saved, redeemed, forgiven, chosen, reconciled'.

I can recall that for weeks and even years after that Spring day, I had a sense of happiness and elation. The love of God was palpable and my life made more sense than it ever had before.

It is the truth that Bethany accepted when she was a child at church. And some version of this theme is what many people interact with when they enter the Christian faith or even other religions.

And, I would argue, it is true. As we discuss Phases Two and Three, the truth that characterizes Phase One will not disappear.

Phase One is always true.

PHASE TWO

I will readily admit that, in my case, Phase One lasted a long time.

The idyllic Phase One lasted at least four years before Phase Two was introduced.

In those four years, I attended a college I loved, began working in ministry, had great friendships, and married a woman whom I admire more than anyone on earth.

To say that it was easy in those four years to believe that *God loved me and had a wonderful plan for my life* would be an understatement.

However, as I would later often tell young people in my ministry, "If you haven't felt real pain yet, just keep breathing."

Pain and problems come for us all.

For me and Kristen, the pain that led us into Phase Two came in a trio of heartbreaks.

First, Kristen experienced a very sad miscarriage.[2]

---

2. Again, for a note on pregnancy/infant/baby loss, see the postscript of this book.

Second, our dreams of going to the mission field became all but impossible—overnight.

Third, we made the painful discovery that not everyone in Christian ministry exhibits the positive characteristics I had expected.

I am well aware that many people have encountered more dynamic difficulties than these. But in our early 20's, it was enough to trigger our entry into Phase Two.

In Phase Two, we have to adjust our beliefs somewhat.

Whereas God's love and plans (basically joy and anticipation) characterize Phase One, God's help as we overcome becomes the theme of our spiritual journey in Phase Two.

Phase Two: God will help you overcome your difficulties and struggles

Inevitably, we face hardships in life.

Sometimes the tough times crop up immediately when we begin our spiritual journey, and so Phase One and Phase Two overlap right away. Other times, we can bask in and experience God's love and favor for an extended time before the road gets too bumpy.

In Phase Two the theme of our spiritual lives is relying on God's help to get through, past, or around our difficulties. The theme verse for Christians in this phase is Romans 8:28, "God will work all things together for the good of those who love him and are called according to his purpose…" This leads to verse 37, in which we are called "more than conquerors through him who loved us."

Our trio of pain that ushered us into Phase Two—the miscarriage and two ministry disappointments—changed our experience of God. I still felt as though God loved me and had plans for me. Phase One hadn't disappeared altogether. But, reeling from experiences that were painful and confusing, I began to rely on God for help. I needed him to comfort me after our loss, and give me direction when our path seemed obscured.

Bethany, her dad, and the rest of her family are in Phase Two. That's why he called and asked everyone to pray. They are asking God to intervene and help them overcome this significant obstacle.

We will discuss Phase Three in the next chapter, but two ancient passages will prepare our hearts now for a discussion to come later. Press pause on our phases as we consider words from Ecclesiastes and Job.

SEASONS

The book of Ecclesiastes contains a well-known passage about times and seasons.[3] It makes for a warm and fuzzy passage if you ignore the more difficult phrases.

For instance, the writer tells us that there is a time to be born and a time to die.

When is it time to die?

What about Bethany?

Certainly, we would not say that it's time for Bethany to die. She's a beautiful young mother with three great kids and you care about her family. Yes, she

---

3. The passage was also made well known by The Byrds in their 1965 chart-topping hit, "Turn! Turn! Turn".

has a serious form of cancer, but treatments can be done right away, and as a young and healthy person otherwise, the possibilities are good that she can overcome this cancer. Phase Two is the appropriate place for Bethany and her family—asking God to help them overcome.

Lessons from Job

Some people believe that the book of Job is the oldest in the Hebrew Bible. It contains the story of a man who has everything stolen from him. His family all dies on the same day. At the same time, many of his friends are killed, his business is ruined, and his possessions are destroyed.

And then even his health is taken from him.

What would you say to Job if you were his friend?

Or the leader of a small religious community in which he participated?

How would you respond to his accumulating grief?

Lessons from Job

I work in a Level II Trauma Center. Our health system has nine hospitals, and my office is in the largest of those facilities. I lead a team of chaplains who respond to some of the most difficult situations that happen in the lives of people in our region.

Chaplains at Parkview respond to every death, every miscarriage and stillbirth, every car accident victim, victims of violence, stroke and heart attack victim, and people who have attempted to take their own lives.

To say that the job is heavy is an understatement. But some days are harder than others.

One day when Chaplain Tom was working, there was a bad car accident near our hospital. A victim came to our Emergency Department (ED). Dylan's work vehicle collided head-on with another on a small country road.[1]

While the man was only minimally conscious before he was whisked away to surgery, he expressed to Chaplain Tom his main concern. His school-age son.

---

1. Names have been changed

Through the beauty of technology, we had information on his family. Tom made the call to the next-of-kin to let them know that Dylan was in the Operating Room at our hospital. That's when he learned some distressing facts.

A year earlier, Dylan's wife, the mother of the son he had mentioned in the ED, had died suddenly and tragically.

Other than his school-age son, Karsten, Dylan's family all lived out of town. Tom asked them to begin traveling our direction, gave them the information he could, and promised a chaplain would be there to receive them when they arrived.

He had no more than hung up the phone when a nurse hung up his phone as well. As their gaze met, Tom knew it wasn't good news.

Dylan had just died.

+++

Karsten's mom died a year previously.

His dad died unexpectedly moments ago.

His closest family was hours away.

What now?

Well, when a patient has died, most chaplains and other healthcare professionals prefer to deliver the news in person if at all possible. In this case, we knew that could not happen in a timely fashion. We also realized another distressing fact: Dylan's son, Karsten, would be out of school before the other family members would be arriving.

Thankfully, when Dylan arrived in our ED, Tom had made one other call. He called the place of worship that was listed in the medical record for Dylan.

Just after Tom had gotten the word of Dylan's death, I met him in our chapel. Two other people were alongside us. The pastor and youth pastor from Dylan and Karsten's church sat in the back pew with Tom. The large chapel, with a two-story ceiling and stained glass windows never seemed so empty.

"Do I call Dylan's dad and tell him what happened?" Tom asked me.

"How far away are they?" I asked.

Tom got them on the phone.

"So, you are about six hours away?" Tom said, glancing in my direction. I nodded. He knew what he had to do.

We teach our chaplains to be direct while being kind.

We use the words *dead, died,* and *death.*

"I'm so sorry to have to tell you that Dylan died in our operating room just moments ago," Tom said to Dylan's dad.

After some final words, Tom got off the phone and we both turned our attention to the pastors from the church.

Their actions are a good model to follow.

"We've already been in touch with the school counselor about the accident," the pastor shared. "We'll go there now, together, and meet the counselor. She will pull Karsten out of class, and we will tell him what happened."

We prayed for them and Karsten, and they bravely set out on what must have been the most difficult drive of their lives.

Several days later a video from the local news grabbed my attention. It was entitled "Community rallies around boy, 12, after death of mother, father".[2]

The story featured three people; Karsten and the two pastors of his church.

Karsten described how everyone had taken care of him, and he shared that although the last year of his life had been sad, it had also been happy (children are so honest). He explained that everyone had been 'his servants'. He seemed pleased about that.

These pastors didn't have any magic words, but they rose to the challenge of meeting this young boy in his pain.

Pain nearly as significant as the pain of Job.

And while many disagree, I believe that the friends of Job in the ancient story provide an example for us, just like these pastors.

2. http://wane.com/2016/05/17/community-rallies-around-boy-12-after-death-of-mother-father/

Job's Friends

If you are familiar with the ancient story of Job, you may have a bias against his friends who come to visit. But they got it right, initially.

> When Job's three friends, Eliphaz the Temanite, Bildad the Shuhite, and Zophar the Naamathite, heard about all the troubles that had come upon him, they set out from their homes and met together by agreement to go and sympathize with him and comfort him. When they saw him from a distance, they could hardly recognize him; they began to weep aloud, and they tore their robes and sprinkled dust on their heads. Then they sat on the ground with him for seven days and seven nights. No one said a word to him, because they saw how great his suffering was. (Job 2:11-13)

These three friends are doing what the rest of us try to do. They are trying to figure out how to act around a friend who has entered their darkest days (truly, as we will see, Job is in Phase Three).

Lessons from Job

You've been there. A friend is diagnosed with a terminal disease. A family member is admitted to Hospice care. Someone in your community is hurt in an accident or an act of violence.

What do you even say?

Job's friends give us four examples to follow.

- *They went.*

They didn't add him to the prayer line.

They met together.

The put a full stop on their 'normal lives' for their friend. They left their own homes. They came together by agreement to go and sympathize with Job. They decided to be with their friend *on purpose.*

When I was in Bible College, I lived nine hours from home. And my roommate one year was a friend who shared my hometown. Ryan and I often carpooled home on breaks from school. And one year, just before finals, we were preparing for another journey home.

I was in the student center one evening when Ryan came in.

I could tell something wasn't right.

Ryan and his grandfather had a close relationship. One of those "go out to lunch, just the two of them" type of friendships. His grandpa had helped him in many ways—financially, relationally, and in ways that sometimes are only possible for grandparents.

Ryan had just gotten off the phone with his mother. This was the old days when you had to pay per minute to talk long distance[3], so calls from home were not as casual then. She shared that his grandfather had a medical event and was in the hospital. They were moving him to comfort care, and he wasn't expected to live more than twenty-four hours.

Ryan was devastated.

He wanted to see his grandfather, but finals were just a couple days away, it was a long drive and his mother had encouraged him to stay and study.

You already know that I wasn't an expert at anything related to visiting the hospital at that age. But there was something in me that knew a conversation was needed.

---

3. Kids, ask your parents

"What do you want to do?" I asked.

Ryan was still in a bit of a shock after hearing the news. "Well, I want to go... but..." he responded.

"Then let's go," I said. A college kid is always up for a sudden adventure.

A small light dawned in his eyes. "You mean, both of us?"

"Sure." I smiled. "I know how to get there..."

Ryan was concerned that even if we left immediately his grandpa might be dead by the time we arrived.

"How about this?" I asked. "How about I drive, since you are dealing with the emotions. I'll set the cruise control at about 23 miles over the speed limit (to avoid getting arrested for reckless driving). Then, if I get pulled over, you can pay for the ticket?" His parents were both accountants, so the plan made a lot of sense to me.[4]

---

4. Kids, don't try this at home. I do not recommend this course of action. Speeding is a serious offense. Our chaplains often tell family members to be careful as they drive to our hospital.

Ryan took me up on the offer, and in about twenty minutes we were in his car and speeding out of town. We encountered exactly zero troopers on our 455-mile trip. The speed limits were lower then. But a trip that usually took us nearly nine hours was completed in six hours and thirty-nine minutes.

I dropped Ryan off at the hospital and went home to sleep.

The next day my phone rang. Ryan was on the other end. He was so thankful for the few hours he got to spend with his grandpa before his death.

Sometimes you just need to go.

Job's friends went.

Dylan and Karsten's pastors went to the school.

Ryan went to be with his grandfather.

Sometimes the best way to help is to put the rest of life on hold and *go*.

Job's friends were silent for seven days.

Lessons from Job

Most of us would die if we had to be silent for seven days. To be honest, as the noise in our lives continues to grow, being silent for seven minutes can seem like a real accomplishment.

Why were they silent? The text says it was because they saw how great his pain was.

Maybe this ancient story is the first place where someone thought, "I don't have any magic words to help you feel better."

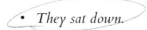

- *They sat down.*

In a 2011 study, the University of Kansas Nursing Department discovered the following:

> Patients perceived the provider [the doctor] as present at their bedside longer when he sat[5], even though the actual time the physician spent at the bedside did not change significantly whether he sat or stood. Patients with whom the physician sat reported a more positive interaction and a better understanding of their condition.[6]

---

5. This isn't a sexist pronoun—all the physicians in their study were male.
6. http://www.pec-journal.com/article/S0738-3991(11)00305-3/fulltext February 2012

All of our chaplains visit a lot of patients at our large hospitals. But some time ago, one stood out among the others. He was regularly visiting 80, even 90 patients in an 8-hour shift. To be fair, he usually works what we call the "rounding shift" where seeing patient after patient is the focus. But others were not seeing that many even when they worked that shift.

I was becoming concerned. Success in caring for the spiritual needs of the sick is not best measured by the speed at which it is accomplished.

So, I asked him. "John, tell me about your visits when you are on the rounding shift."

"I go in. I sanitize my hands. I introduce myself. I ask if I can sit down. If they say yes, I pull the chair up close to the side of the bed. I look them in the eyes and listen for a little while. I ask if they need prayer. I wish them well. I sanitize my hands again, and I head to the next room."

Perfect. Although looking at his numbers, I was concerned, I guarantee the patients didn't feel rushed when this compassionate, older man was sitting and looking into their eyes.

Lessons from Job

And, to be overly practical, it has a lot to do with sitting down.

Eliphaz and Job's other two friends must have referenced the University of Kansas study. Or else, they must have intuitively been able to feel that since Job was in such rough shape, they needed to sit with him—literally.

Sometimes you need to go, sit down and be quiet.

- *They wept out loud.*

I am not a crier.

At one point in my life, I thought that was something to be proud of. I looked down on those who cried 'too much' and I considered them weak. This misunderstanding of people (and the nature of crying) nearly cost me my relationship with my beautiful bride!

But I have learned better.

When my ministry was focused on young people, we took a trip each summer to a church camp with high school students. I looked forward to it every year.

But one year everything broke loose in the middle of the week.

We received word that there had been a bad car accident and two young men (friends of many in our youth group) had tragically died. I didn't know the boys personally, but they were very much a part of the lives of many of the students I cared about.

Many of the plans for the rest of the week were adjusted. The adult leaders, myself included, spent a lot of time listening, talking, and praying with the kids who were the most affected.

One night, we were singing in the main service. A small group of teens was in the row in front of me. They had their arms around one another. They were crying quietly. And I got caught up thinking about them (sympathizing with them). I reached up and placed a hand of support on the young man right in front of me.

That's when it happened.

I started to cry. Not for the boys who had died. I couldn't do that—I didn't even know them.

But I cried for the pain my friends were in.

Lessons from Job

As teens usually do, they welcomed me into their circle and put their arms around me as well.

Later, one student told me that he learned more about God from the tears I shed in that circle that evening than from all of my Sunday school lessons combined.

I'm still not sure if that was a compliment. But I am sure it was true.

People ask what chaplains do at the hospital. I describe being present for 40% of the deaths in our entire region, delivering death notifications, praying over dying loved ones and serving victims of everything from strokes to gun violence. I get some common questions.

How do you do it?

Isn't that depressing?

But the truly sensitive people ask another question.

Is it ok for you to cry?

In our work, we have a specific answer to this question. When I give you this answer, you have to remember that we are working in a professional environment, not as pastors of a congregation, as friends of the grieving, or as family of the sick.

Our answer is twofold. First, the answer is, "Of course. If you didn't occasionally cry over such heartbreak, you would no longer be a human being." Secondly, we remember that this situation is not about us. It's not our loved one who has died. It's not our mom in the bed. It's not our son who was shot or our daughter who overdosed on drugs. That way, we keep any tears focused on the patient and family, not on ourselves.

Maybe you are good at crying. When my wife, Kristen, heard that there were people in the first century who could be hired to mourn at funerals to show respect for the dead, her response was, "I think I could do that job."

That was not my response.

But, I think Job's friends give us a good example to follow. When someone close to us is in that much pain, crying out loud is an appropriate response.

Lessons from Job

Let's summarize the examples we have uncovered in Job's story:

- They went
- They sat down
- They shut up
- They cried

We are, slowly, wading into what we will later speak of more directly.

We are entering Phase Three.

Go, sit down, shut up, and cry.

Simple, right? Yes, it is simple. But it's not always easy. Sometimes our inclinations lead us very far from these simple practices, especially when people are in Phase Three. We'll discuss these in chapter five.

When we move from Phase Two to Phase Three, we begin to sense that we will no longer overcome. Certainly, I think, Job had given up on overcoming—at least in any sense he had been familiar with previously.

What do we do when we begin to realize that we will no longer overcome?

That God won't help us past or through this difficulty?

God may be helping us, but not in the way we had hoped. He's not fixing the problem.

I am not sure it would have helped Job for his friend, Zophar, to say, "God loves you and has a wonderful plan for your life."

And if Bildad had told Job, "Romans 8:28 buddy. God is going to work this for your good. You are more than a conqueror…" I predict that would have fallen on deaf ears.

Phase One and Two themes fail when we enter Phase Three.

Sometimes, it's not about what we are *doing* for someone in Job's or Ryan's or Karsten's situation.

Sometimes, it's about just being there.

And that can feel like doing *nothing*.

I DID NOTHING

One day a woman rolled through the front door of my office. She stopped at the assistant's office, chatted, then came back to my office. This elderly woman has been a patient many times but is also one of our hospital volunteers in the cancer center. She uses a motorized scooter and has had her share of health problems. After she left, my assistant came down to my office.

"What did you do for her?" She asked, looking confused.

"I'm not sure what you mean?" I replied.

"She told me that the last time she was in the hospital—when you came to see her—that you saved her life." Her mouth was open and she was looking over her reading glasses waiting to hear some amazing story of my pastoral care or spiritual intervention in her life.

I wanted to live up to her expectations.

But I had to be honest.

"Um, just listened, I guess." Her mouth closed, she looked at me sideways and headed to the workroom. She either thought I was lying or that I was even more unimpressive than she had previously believed.

HOW TO TALK

You see, this patient, a friend whose religion doesn't match my own, was in a dark place in the hospital. She had called my assistant and asked if "Pat" could come. She is one of the only people in the world who gets away with calling me "Pat". I've been "Patrick" since the first grade.

So, Pat went over to her room. While her medical situation was not good, she was more concerned with issues of grief and relationships in her family. She told me some things that made me sad.

I sat in the vinyl-covered floral-print chair, the smell of hospital in the air. I greeted the nurses who needed to interrupt our conversation a few times.

I held her hand.

I looked her in the eye.

I sympathized.

Which is basically to say that I did *nothing*. But it was everything to her.

Teresa taught me this lesson early in my career at the hospital.

Lessons from Job

When I was interviewing to be a chaplain, I shadowed Teresa, an experienced chaplain. I followed her around, just like a shadow, and went from room to room, bowed my head when she prayed, and that was about it.

Later, when I got the job, she said, "I told everyone that after our four hours together, I knew you would be a good chaplain."

"But I didn't do anything," I was genuinely confused.

With a wink, she said, "Exactly."

Go.

Sit down.

Be quiet.

Cry.

I discuss these concepts in more detail in my 20 part YouTube series. Search for Patrick and Kristen Riecke on YouTube and select the playlist entitled "Course: How to talk with Sick, Dying, and Grieving People". Subscribe today.

Ch. 4 How to Visit the Hospital

Visiting the hospital can be intimidating. It feels like going to another country where a different language is spoken, the people wear different attire, and the smells are unfamiliar. I am sorry to say that I have known many people, even clergy, who avoid the hospital at all costs. One pastor, after he mustered the courage to drive to our hospital campus, circled the large facility several times. Then, his courage failed. He could not manage to park and enter the facility to visit the person on his list that day.

I've already admitted to you that I've felt this way before. Maybe you have, too. Are there certain things we can *always*, *sometimes*, or *never* do to make sure our hospital visit helps the patient? Certainly. Let's begin with seven things you should *always* do when you visit a hospital. (These tips are also listed on a simple wallet card that you can request for free at PatrickRiecke.com.)

ALWAYS

1. Call Ahead

Navigating a modern hospital can be like arriving at an airport. The main campus of the health system I serve has sixteen main entrances and dozens of smaller doors. Even our smaller community hospitals have multiple entrances. When you call the hospital, ask to speak with a nurse for the patient you are coming to see. Don't only secure the room number, but ask by which door you should enter, and which elevators. This is also a good time to make sure you are respecting any visiting hours or restrictions that may apply. As we have discovered in 2020, rules and restrictions can change drastically from time to time. If you skip this step, you will find yourself focused on the navigation of a hospital campus and hospital rules instead of caring at the beginning of your hospital visit.

2. Go to the Hospital

This is obvious, but you actually have to *go* to the hospital. In our busy lives, it can be easy for things to fall through the cracks. I can't tell you how many times friends, family, and clergy have faltered at this step. My encouragement is *always* to *go*.

3. Sanitize Your Hands

Nurses and other health care workers sanitize their hands hundreds of times a shift. It is *the* most basic aspect of good health care. You should be no different. You want what's best for that person in the hospital, too. While I know that *wash your hands* sounds more like a grandmother's advice than it does good care for the sick, dying, and grieving, good hand hygiene does more than prevent disease. It communicates respect. It says to the person, "I value you enough to be sure I am not bringing in anything that could harm you further." I take a spray of sanitizer as I walk into a patient room, and I make sure I am still rubbing the solution through my fingers when I approach the patient. After all, I will certainly want to clean my hands on the way out. If the patient sees me using the sanitizer *only* when I walk out, what am I communicating to her? She may feel that I value my own health more than I value hers. Health care has a saying: "Clean hands in, clean hands out." You should *always* do the same.

4. Sit Down

Remember Job's friends? Remember the study from the University of Kansas nursing department that we discovered in the last chapter? Ask the patient, "Is it ok if I sit down?" Then be careful where you sit. Pull up an empty chair. Don't sit on the bed. Try to sit in a way that you can make easy eye contact without the patient needing to strain their body position. This will always prepare you to have a good visit.

5. Just Listen

Being silent in the presence of another is a skill you must develop. All our chaplains at our health care system do this well. It's actually quite difficult. After you've said hello, you feel the urge to say *something.* To make sense of the situation. To ask questions. To remind them of certain promises of God. The desire to speak can feel like being underwater and needing to breathe. If you feel you need to say something, try this. Count slowly from ten to one. Take a deep breath. Then do it again. Pray a prayer silently. And remember that Job's friends were silent for seven days and seven nights. Surely you can be silent for seven minutes. The conversation at the hospital is different than the conversation at the grocery store. The person might be in pain, on medication, or just in deep thought about their situation. Blurting a few words that make you feel better and rushing out the door won't help. *Always* practice silence and listening when you visit the hospital.

6. Keep it Private

Not only does HIPAA federal law prevent you from sharing protected health information in the United States and other countries, but it's also a matter of respect. I'm sorry to say that I have often heard pastors tell very intimate details about a person's health when they should have kept it private. Better yet, ask the person or family member if they want to be placed on the prayer line, how they feel about others knowing, or if the information is public (on social media, etc.). Treat their information like you would the news that a woman is pregnant. It's her news to share *with whom* she so desires and *when* she desires to share it. Patients may also want *some* details shared about their situation but not others. Don't take that right away from the patient.

7. Keep it Short

A hospital room is a busy place. The sicker the patient is, the busier the room will be. Your visit is important. If the patient wants to talk, then stay and listen as long as necessary. Otherwise, don't overstay your welcome. Just like you should always keep information private, plan to keep your visit short.

SOMETIMES

Now that we have discovered seven things we should *always* do when we visit a hospital, let's consider four things we should *sometimes* do that can make a big difference.

1. Stay Until the End

I mean two things when I say that you should *sometimes* stay until the end. First, I mean to stay until an event is over. Maybe it's a surgery or test. Maybe they came into the emergency department and are waiting for a diagnosis or admission. It can sometimes bring comfort to the family or patient if you stay until the end of that event. When it's known that the patient is stable, or out of surgery, that a good time for a support person to exit. There's seldom a need for you to visit the patient himself after surgery. He probably won't remember the visit anyhow.

Secondly, I mean to stay until the end of the person's life. We will discuss the moment of death in a later chapter. For now, suffice it to say that it can *sometimes* be very meaningful for you to stay until the person has died.

2. Be an Advocate

It's a pretty safe bet that nearly every patient in the hospital is tired. And when they are tired, it can become more difficult for them to ask for what they need. The patient you are visiting might need his nurse to come in. Or he might need a pillow to help him become more comfortable. You can advocate for him by simply hitting the call button or asking staff for what he needs. However, what if he has bigger needs? What if he is not getting along with his doctor? Or he feels the nurse isn't listening to his real needs? Or he's worried about having what he needs when he leaves the hospital? You can advocate for these needs as well. He has a right to good communication with his care team, and to feel safe when he is discharged.

I know one quiet and peaceful pastor who became an advocate during a hospital visit. The doctor rounded on the patient while he was making a pastoral visit. The physician dumped some pretty difficult news on the patient, sped through some complicated information, and spun on his heel to leave. My mild-mannered friend tracked the doctor down in the hallway and tapped him on the shoulder. He said, "I don't know what just happened in there, but your patient needs a little more of your time. We have more questions." The doctor was shocked that he hadn't communicated well. After all, he gave them lots of information. Because my friend was willing to advocate for the patient, the doctor came back into the room, sat down, and took all the time the patient needed. *Sometimes* we need to advocate for people who may lack the ability to speak up for themselves.

3. Ask Deep Questions

Everyone is asking the patient how they are feeling physically. Their physical health is the topic of nearly every interaction. When you visit a patient, you could ask her how she is doing emotionally. Say something like, "I imagine I would feel pretty overwhelmed if I were you. How are you holding up?" Again, medical crises can also be crises of faith.

Sometimes you need to ask, "What are you praying for right now?" That's a deeper question than "When do you think you will be discharged?"

On a phone call with a coworker recently, I just asked him "How are you doing with all this?" It was an open-ended question that allowed him to talk at length about the toll a recent violent death had taken on him.

Beyond emotional and spiritual questions, relationship struggles can become central during a health crisis. Asking a simple question like "Has your family been visiting?" can invite a patient to discuss relationship dynamics that their nurse may not discover. *Sometimes* we need to ask deep questions.

4. Refer to Another Professional

Let me give you good news. You don't have to solve all the problems of a hospitalized person. If they divulge feelings to you that include mental health or financial needs, transportation or housing shortfalls, or transitional healthcare placement questions, you can refer them to other professionals. Talk with the social worker, case manager, or chaplain. Make a couple of calls for them to see who can help. You don't have to do it all. Making some connections for them could make a big difference.

NEVER

This is my favorite part of the list. These are seven things you should *never* do when you visit a patient in the hospital.

1. Force Prayer

Should you pray for people in the hospital? Of course. If you are a praying person, you should *always* pray for people in the hospital. However, should you pray *out loud* and *in person*? It depends. Here's how you will know. Simply ask if they would like prayer. In my experience, you can expect one of three responses. First, they may say yes, and shift in their bed. That means they want you to pray out loud and in person, and you should do it now. Second, they may say, "I'd be happy to be on the prayer list," or "Keep me in your prayers." That means they don't mind the idea of prayer, but they don't want to do it now. That could simply mean that they aren't feeling great, they are tired, or they want to call the nurse to help them to the bathroom. In that case, it's time to leave and you can pray as you walk out of the hospital. Third, they may ignore your question about prayer altogether. This may indicate that they are struggling with what to think about God while they are sick or injured. For this group, forcing prayer could be a big mistake.

I make this analogy. Kristen and I have four children. When they were young they would often hurt or offend one another, as siblings do. Their mom and I would force them to apologize to one another. After all, we are good parents, right? However, you can imagine how those forced apologies usually went. They were quick, insincere, and usually still full of anger and frustration. Did the forced apology reconcile the relationship? No. And forced prayer doesn't improve the patient's relationship with God, either. It can actually do damage. That's why you should *never* force prayer when visiting a patient in the hospital.

2. Be Afraid to Cry

When people outside of the hospital hear what chaplains do, they ask some common questions. One common question is, "Do you ever cry when you are serving a family whose loved one just died?" The answer, of course, is *yes*. The day that violence, sickness, cancer, miscarriage, stillbirth, strokes, heart attacks, and death can no longer bring tears to our eyes is the day we should quit being hospital chaplains. I could tell a hundred stories about crying with families. While it is important that I don't make the situation about myself and my own sadness, shedding some tears with the family can build a meaningful bridge between myself and them. I no longer apologize for crying, and neither should you. *Never* be afraid to cry.

3. Interrogate the Patient

You don't need to know every detail of their diagnosis, what medicine they took, how long they have had this disease, etc. Those details matter much less than you might imagine. Resist the urge to ask if they have tried this or that remedy or treatment to regain their health. Being admitted to the hospital involves a mountain of data and information. No patient can be expected to remember it all. Remember that you can sometimes ask deep questions that only have a small amount to do with their physical health. Resist the urge to ask a million questions. Sometimes the reason you want to ask is to be sure that the fate that has befallen the patient won't happen to you or a loved one. That is a self-focused approach that won't help the patient you are seeing today. Therefore, *never* interrogate the patient about their condition.

4. Question their Faith

People with serious illnesses or injuries are learning more about trusting God than anyone else. And no amount of belief in God magically makes a person healthy. Ed Dobson, the late pastor and author, died of ALS. In one of his last sermons, one he preached alongside his son, Kent, Dobson painfully addressed this common mistake. Through extremely garbled speech due to the ALS, Dobson said, "People keep telling me to trust God. I want to ask them, 'What do you think I am trying to do?'" Please, *never* question the faith of the patient during a hospital visit.

5. Belittle Clinicians

We will talk later about the danger of painting a medical situation as God versus the doctors. While I encourage you to *sometimes* become an advocate for the patient, and even have hard conversations with clinicians, that doesn't mean speaking poorly of them or vilifying them. Remember that after you leave, those nurses and doctors, and others will continue to care for the patient. Therefore, *never* disparage the clinicians.

6. Assume that You Understand

Maybe you had an aunt who had cancer. That does not mean that you understand what obstacles face every other person with cancer. Even more painfully, just because your dad died doesn't mean that you fully understand when *her* dad dies. Never say, "I know how you feel." You don't. Just as no one can understand your grief or fear completely, you cannot understand theirs. Instead, you could say, "If I were you, I might feel scared." That communicates that you are trying to put yourself in their shoes, not just giving advice you think they need. *Never* assume that you understand.

7. Assume that You Know What God Will Do

I've made this mistake in both directions. I've been sure that a person is at the end of life and they lived for several more years. I've also been sure that a patient is fine and they have died shortly thereafter.

Less than twenty-four hours ago I was in a hospital room with a family. They were gathered around the patient's bed. Several children and their spouses as well as the patient's spouse made a semi-circle around her. I stood behind them, handing out tissues. The care team was preparing to remove her ventilator. The family was there to say goodbye.

The pastor from the patient's church stood in the front of the family, at the foot of her bed. He tried to maintain silence after we all entered the room, but he didn't make it five minutes. He read scripture about not being troubled and how we would all be together again in heaven. He prayed a long prayer about God welcoming her into eternity *now*, and how she would receive the promise of eternal life *today*. His prayer was a goodbye message.

That was twenty-four hours ago. The vent was removed just after his prayer. The family stood and watched and waited for their mother and wife to enter eternity. However, as I write these words, she is still breathing. Still struggling. Her last breath will likely come soon, but who knows? Only God knows.

After the pastor prayed his prayer, he left so quickly that I found his bible left behind. He was uncomfortable and trying to provide comfort. I have felt that feeling before, too. Once he was gone, I warned the family that after the vent was out things could happen quickly. "However," I told them, "you never know. Sometimes it can take quite a long time."

Never pretend you know what God will do.

If these actions to *always, sometimes,* or *never* take when you visit a person in the hospital are helpful to you, go to PatrickRiecke.com/resources to request your free wallet card. It lists all these actions in brief form as reminders for you when you visit. You can also find several videos on the topics in this chapter over at our YouTube channel by searching for Patrick and Kristen Riecke.

Phase Three and The Moment of Death

PHASE THREE

When I present a day-long workshop on this material, there is always one participant who comes up before lunch and says something like "I think I missed something earlier. I wrote down Phase One of our spiritual lives–*God loves me and has a wonderful plan for my life*, and Phase Two is *God will help me overcome my difficulties in this world*, but what is Phase Three?"

They usually have a pen in hand, ready to write the phrase in their notes.

But we don't come to Phase Three in life easily or quickly.

Before I share the statement that I believe best describes Phase Three, remember that when we reach Phase Three, we do not leave Phase One and Two altogether. In other words, God still loves us and has a plan for our lives. Our definition of that truth might have changed significantly, but it remains true. Likewise, God will still help us through our difficulties. Again, just not in the way we initially thought. These two phases sometimes take on greater meaning when we embrace Phase Three.

Simply put, Phase Three is when God brings meaning out of our suffering.

Would we like to avoid suffering?

Of course.

Once we are suffering, would we like to escape?

Of course.

But when we cannot escape the suffering, does that mean that our lives are meaningless?

Of course not.

Many people have found that suffering without relief, while they would not choose it, has brought the greatest meaning to life. And we will discover those opportunities in case studies over the next few chapters.

I would also say, as a Christian pastor, the tragic death of Jesus is perhaps the greatest religious example of God bringing meaning out of suffering. It would be hard to imagine more suffering than being betrayed, tortured, and murdered in front of your mother and a crowd of people.

Yet, God seems to say that he is bringing immense meaning from the suffering of Jesus.

These two principles—that many people find meaning in suffering and the Cross of Jesus—came together for me in one of the most dynamic experiences in my ministry.

MEANING IN SUFFERING

Several years ago a good friend asked me if I would have lunch with her step-dad. He was very sick with cancer. He nearly died once already—more about that in a minute.

It was especially hard because he was a young man—only a decade older than myself.

I get requests like this occasionally—requests to talk with people I don't know when they are facing death or other life-altering situations. While extremely meaningful, they can be intimidating. I can have the feeling that the person sitting across from me wants me to make sense of age-old questions like "is there life after death?" or "why am I suffering?" or, the most difficult question, "why do bad things happen to good people?"

Fortunately for me, Tony just wanted to talk.

He wanted to tell me stories.

Stories of things he had thought, felt, realized, and seen through his cancer battle.

One story stuck with me.

Coming out of a cancer surgery that had been very difficult, he had a vision. In the vision, he was flying. He was soaring through the bluest sky over a beautiful paradise.

"The colors…" he looked off over my shoulder, as though he was having the vision all over again. "They were so…" he paused again because he wanted the next word to sum up his entire vision.

"Vivid. I didn't want to come back. I wanted to stay in that place. And when I woke up after the surgery, I was mad. I wanted to go back."

It was at this moment that I realized he was helping me more than I was helping him (that continued until his death).

Tony and I met several more times, and we discovered that both of us are very task-oriented people. We start and end each day with a to-do list. At least, he used to.

"Lately, though," Tony said, "I don't do things just to get them done anymore. Now I do them for the experience. To slow down. To savor. To enjoy."

I confessed to Tony that I was reading a particular book at the time just to finish the book. In light of what he was telling me, I realized how stupid that was. I ought to read a book to *read* it, not to *finish* it. As though I get some kind of points for finishing that task.

Meaning out of Suffering

We were in the parking lot that day, outside the pizza buffet restaurant where we enjoyed lunch. Tony, in his grey suit with a blue tie, gave me a little grin again as we parted ways, "Now go finish that book."

A few months later, Tony was homebound. He and his wife lived in my neighborhood. I stopped by from time to time. Eventually, he went on hospice care.

One day, Tony was no longer himself. The cancer was getting the best of him, and he was having a hard time making sense of the world around him.

His family stepped out of his room while I stayed with him at his bedside. I read to him about the New Heaven and the New Earth. About how there would no longer be any pain. No more sickness. No more tears. About how God writes our names in his book. I wasn't trying to focus only on the afterlife, but he was in pain and needed something to look forward to.

In his struggle for being awake and aware, he said the only words he could muster.

"I like that book… I like that book… I like that book."

HOW TO TALK

I remembered our conversation in Pizza Hut months before when his eyes sparkled as he kidded me about finishing my book.[1] Time has a funny way of slowing down at a time like this.

As I helped him drink a cup of soda, I held the straw to his lips.

What happened next, I cannot explain.

Before my eyes, Tony's face transformed into the face of Christ.

Not 'feed-the-five-thousand' or 'walk-on-the-water' Jesus. But 'dying on the cross struggling to communicate' Jesus.

And I was the one offering him a drink.

I didn't know it, but there would be a lot more times that I would be at a person's bedside at the time of death. That I would lead a team of people who do this work daily. To be honest, I probably didn't even know such a team existed.

---

1. Tony was a good example of what I talk about in How to Find Meaning in Your Life Before it Ends

Meaning out of Suffering

Tony had learned how to enjoy, how to savor. He taught me that every person is Jesus. That when we look at the dying person in the bed, that we can see the face of God every time.

Would Tony have liked to avoid the suffering of cancer at a young age?

Of course.

Once he was suffering, would he have liked to escape?

Of course.

Did his suffering mean his life was meaningless?

Of course not.

If I could change the past, I would make sure that Tony didn't die from cancer one-hundred times out of one-hundred. But since none of us could change what was happening, bringing meaning out of his suffering offered a small piece of redemption.

How God brings meaning out of suffering is a mystery.

But it a mystery often experienced.

DEATH IS A SACRED MOMENT

The first time I presented this material a participant approached me at a break. "Are you going to talk about how death is a sacred moment?"

Although it wasn't in my notes that day, this is a basic truth of every death—whether sudden or expected. Every person who dies is breathing one moment and in the next—they are dead.

Tony's moment came in a hospice home in our city. And it was, indeed a sacred moment.

The family had called, feeling Tony was in his last hours.

They were right.

I didn't know at that time that most people aren't able to interact much with those around them in the hours before death. Between their waning capacities, sickness. and medicine, it creates a fog too thick to break through.

But when I walked in Tony's room—a friend I had known for only a year—he looked up at me and said, "Patrick!"

Meaning out of Suffering

It was the only word I heard him say in that room. And you could have knocked me over with a feather when he did.

As a pastor, you want to help people.

The rest of that day, there was no real help to offer.

I sat near the family, near Tony. I don't remember if I ever prayed—though I probably did.

I know that I cried and that I held Tony's hand.

Just like there are no magic words to help someone in Phase Three, there are no perfect words to describe how sacred the moment of death is.

But if you have been there—you know.[2]

---

2. If you are doing the funeral, I recommend Dr. Jon Swanson's book, *Giving a Life Meaning*

Leader Roles
- *Phase 1* — Announcing the good news - coming into faith
- *Phase 2* — Teaching & Nurturing - growing in the faith
- *Phase 3* — Lead the Conversation, Represent God

ch.6

The Role of Faith Leaders

Remember that the theme of Phase One of our spiritual lives is *God loves you and has a wonderful plan for your life.* What is the role of a faith leader in Phase One? It's announcing the news. The faith leader is the one giving the message, "God cares, and has plans for you."

You will also remember that in Phase Two of our spiritual lives the theme is *God will help you overcome your difficulties.* The faith leader's role in this phase is teaching and nurturing. We are helping people to grow in their faith and their trust in God. Friends play a similar role, cheering the person on through their struggle—always with an expectation that they will overcome.

Helpers

However, what do we call it when we will no longer overcome in this life? How do we describe our spiritual lives in that usually thin sliver of time when we know the person will not recover, and that the end of their life is imminent? Or maybe it is becoming obvious that what they hoped and prayed for is not going to happen. In Phase Three what is the role of a faith leader, or a friend who cares about the person's spiritual life?

Many of you reading these words *are* those friends or faith leaders. You need to hear how important your role is as people approach Phase Three. In the distant past, the role of the clergy person was primary when a person was seriously ill, approaching death, and certainly after the person had died. Today, we can downplay this important role, deferring to physicians and other clinicians. But in Phase Three, it may be time for the person of faith to lead the conversation.

This came home to me in a simple story one of my chaplains shared with me. Chaplain Dianna was new to our department. The hospital she was assigned to is small—with only a few dozen inpatient beds. She was making her rounds, knocking on each patient's door, and visiting. But when she knocked on one particular door, just in front of one of the larger stations for nurses, the patient inside responded that she could not visit right now. Chaplain Dianna responded, "It's okay, it's just the chaplain."

Just the chaplain.

If you are a leader in a faith community, maybe you sometimes feel this way when you are involved in caring for a person who is sick, injured, newly diagnosed, or in grief. You may think to yourself, "I'm not the doctor," or "I'm not a counselor."

Let me put it this way. When we need a doctor, we need a doctor. A friend, chaplain, or clergy member won't do.

But when we need a friend, chaplain, or clergy member, our doctor won't do.

We each have a place at the table as we care for people in their most difficult times.

As the chair of the ethics committee for my health system, I often have a front-row seat to some of the most complicated scenarios at our hospitals. These usually involve either the beginning of life (pregnancy can be quite complicated) or the end of life.

Helpers

Sadly, sometimes the beginning of life and the end of life come together.[1]

This was going to be the case for one mom and baby whose situation I had been following. Mom was bound to deliver too early for our NICU to intervene. One day, as I left the office, the word was that she was in active labor and would deliver at any time.

The next morning, I checked her chart for an update. I expected to see information on her file about the stillbirth.

But I didn't.

I was sure she had delivered in the twelve hours I had been away from the facility. Then it dawned on me.

If the baby wasn't dead when he was born, I would need to look in a different location—not in mom's chart.

That's when I discovered the smallest, saddest, most beautiful little medical record I have ever seen.

---

1. For a touching song on this topic, listen to Smallest Wingless by Craig Cardiff

This little one lived for a very short period after birth—less than one hour. At that time, no clinical care was administered. There was none to offer—the little one was just too small for all available instruments.

But care had been provided.

There were only two healthcare professionals who had documented in this tiny medical record.

They were both chaplains.

Their notes, of course, didn't describe body temperature, blood pressure, or heart rate. They described the emotional and spiritual support that was offered. Sacraments performed. Information is given. Documentation made so we could follow up later for bereavement. Funeral home selected.

It is unlikely anyone else will ever review that tiny chart again. Not since I did the day after this baby was born (and died). Even the chaplains who wrote the notes will have no reason to revisit them at any point. There was almost no point to even record those notes because no one was ever going to see them.

Except I did.

Invisible Helpers

I did see the notes of the care provided by our chaplains at the time of birth and death for this precious baby.

Often, what we do for those in their darkest times, whether we are faith leaders or friends, is invisible.

But the ultimate meaning is often invisible.

No one stands up and cheers when you let the grieving mother cry on your shoulder. No one gives you an award for sitting vigil at the bed of an unresponsive patient. No one writes a story about the family who drops off a meal and a hug to a family who is facing cancer.

Often, no one even knows.

Often, like our two chaplains, your notes will never be reviewed. They will never be seen.

Except God sees.

More than that, I think God is looking for these little actions *more* than those actions that win awards, garner attention, or have stories written about them.

I'm not sure what the afterlife looks like (more on the afterlife in chapter five), but I have a feeling that when those two chaplains arrive there, God may have these two little notes in hand, with tear-stained eyes, and they may hear the words, "Thank you. Well done."

Don't let the invisibility of what you are doing to help the hurting discourage you. You are not *just* their friend. Not *just* the person from the faith community. You have a significant place at the table.

Remember, when we need a friend, a doctor just won't do.

When God needs a representative, it could be you.

5 Mistakes to Avoid in Phase Three

There's a good chance that one of the reasons you picked up this book is because you had an experience similar to the ones I described in the opening pages. You found yourself, perhaps unexpectedly, in the presence of someone who was suffering greatly, and you didn't know what to say. You didn't know how to help.

This is one of the most difficult moments we ever face. We care about the person who is experiencing this overwhelming pain, and we naturally want to do something that will help. But our usual tools—the tools that work well when people are in Phase One or Two of their journey—are useless now.

Even offering to pray for a person who is in one of these moments can seem a bit like trying to use a wrench when the job calls for a screwdriver—it's just not the right tool. This has historically been a struggle especially for people of faith like me. We tend to rehash the words we say at other times of life. That can hurt our friends who are going through a hard time. To learn more about these phases, what to say, and what not to say, check out my online videos on my YouTube channel (search Patrick and Kristen Riecke). I'd also be happy to talk with you about coming to speak to your group in person.

DANGEROUS INCLINATIONS

Below is a brief discussion of five natural inclinations for those of us who want to help a person during a difficult time. But they are dangerous for the people we are helping. Perhaps it's our way to grasp for magic words. If you find yourself alongside someone in a lot of pain, try to avoid these five common mistakes:

1. Defending God

As the leader of a large team of chaplains, I do what leaders usually do. I go to meetings, answer emails, and perform other administrative and leadership tasks.

Phase Three

But sometimes, I get the call, and I am intimately involved with the care of a patient or family who is in a dark time.

One such day, one of our chaplains called me because he had been paged to two deaths at the same time. The patients' rooms on opposite sides of the building and their time of death was almost the same. He was in the ED with one of the families. The other patient had died in our cancer unit, which is near my office.

I offered to see the patient in the cancer unit. I also knew, as all our chaplains know, that deaths in the cancer unit are usually a bit easier from our standpoint. No one expects a person to die in the ED (not even the staff). But the cancer hospital unit is different. Families have had more time to prepare—usually. As such, they know what funeral home they are going to use, the appropriate family is already on-site, and they have usually even done some of their grieving before the patient's death. In this unit, death comes as less of a shock… *usually.*

My visit to this family started in the usual way. The patient wasn't old but wasn't young either. The family at the bedside shared how long ago the diagnosis had been delivered. They also shared that her husband was on his way—he had not been there at the time of her death.

When he arrived, it became clear that this was not going to be a simple situation after all.

The man's emotion and volume began to escalate immediately when he entered the room. And he wasn't just sad. He was angry. Not angry at the staff or me or his family or his wife.

He was angry at God.

He began yelling at the sky. He shook his fist. He sobbed.

"Why, God?" is a question many of us ask during these times. It's just that most of us keep this question buried in our hearts, making us sick from the inside out.

This man didn't keep the question inside. He was yelling—loudly. He also didn't stay inside his wife's room. He started walking the hall, yelling at God.

I started wishing that I was in the ED with the other family.

Phase Three

Little did I know how difficult this was going to be.

There I was, walking with him up and down the hall of this unit full of other patients and staff while he was screaming at the heavens.

Inside, I felt some responses rising— "Sir, your wife wasn't elderly, but it seems you had a long life together." Or, "Your brother-in-law said you have known she had a terminal condition for several months, how can you be so surprised?" But most of all, "God didn't kill your wife, he gave you your wife for many decades. Cancer is what took her life, not God."

And, remember, the only thing he knew about me was that my name was Patrick, and I was a chaplain.

So, what did I say to him?

Not much.

I just walked with him, listened to him, and kept saying, "I'm so sorry."

Why?

HOW TO TALK

Emotional Questions

Because his question was an emotional one—and quite a natural response. To respond with a logical answer would not have helped him. Perhaps he could have had a logical conversation later. Probably months later. At that time maybe someone could have said some of those things I felt rising inside of me. But twenty minutes after his wife died was not the right time to defend God.

Defending God is one of the natural inclinations at a time like this.

Let me be more honest.

We incline to defend our understanding of God and faith, life, and death.

But we have to ask ourselves, "Am I defending God, my faith, my point of view, as a way of helping this person, or justifying my internal thinking and belief?" If it's the latter, then we are helping ourselves, not the person in their dark time.

2. Teaching Theology
Similar to defending God, sometimes we are inclined to teach theology to people who are in pain. We want to tell them what our faith says about times of difficulty, or about how God is good all the time,

even when it doesn't feel that way. These things may be true, but we are making a mistake when we follow this inclination.

Again, their questions at this time are usually emotional, not theological, such as "If God is good, why is he doing this to me?". When we give a theological answer to an emotional question, we aren't communicating. We aren't helping.

3. Only focusing on the afterlife

I hope you have never had to go to a funeral where someone stood up and told everyone there not to be sad because the person was in heaven. Even if the family and friends are 100% sure that the person is enjoying an eternal life of extreme bliss, trying to tell someone not to be sad, for any reason, seldom helps them.

For several months, my daughter was plagued by night terrors. Not simply nightmares, but night terrors. If you have ever been around someone having a night terror, you know the difference. It's like a combination of sleepwalking and a nightmare and multiplied by ten.

HOW TO TALK

A couple of hours after we put her to bed, she would wake up screaming uncontrollably. She would repeat one or two words over and over, usually "Mommy..." followed by another word or phrase. At first, we would try to wake her up and tell her everything was ok. Every time she would call for me or my wife, we would tell her we were there and ask what she needed. We would try to reassure her and ask her what was wrong. She could never respond to these attempts to communicate.

We bought a camera for her room so we could see what was precipitating these episodes.

The answer—nothing.

She would just wake up with her tears flowing, chin quivering and flailing about.

When we realized she was having night terrors we changed our approach.

We no longer tried to dialogue with her much. We didn't get as frustrated with her. We didn't ask her what was wrong. We just tried to be close to her, give her what she needed, and wait it out. Usually, in about ten minutes she would be able to go back to sleep.

Trying to convince my daughter that 'everything was okay' during these episodes is similar to trying to tell the grieving that everything is okay because their loved one is in heaven. It might be true, but it's not helpful.

Notice, the danger here is *only* focusing on the afterlife. Considering the afterlife is important, but if it is our only tool to try to help someone, we will find that we are not helping that much.

I often speak to groups on these topics. Sometimes those groups are staff at a healthcare agency, sometimes they are community members, and sometimes they are connected with a faith community.

One time while speaking to a group that was mostly comprised of faith leaders, one experienced pastor said something I have heard many times. "I have always seen that Christian people approach death much differently than people with no faith. They have peace and assurance that they are going to be with Jesus." And while I somewhat wish this was true (as a Christian clergy person), it certainly is not *always* true. As the leader of the workshop, I didn't want to shoot down one of the participants.

Fortunately, a couple of my other chaplains were in the room. Jon raised his hand and carefully shared that he found that even people who had great faith seemed to sometimes still be scared to die, and their loved ones were just as sad to see them die.

4. Cheering people up

Again, young people usually understand the emotional nature of difficult times better than the more mature among us. I can remember a young man who was a part of my youth group years ago. When he learned that a good friend's mom had died, he told us all he just wanted to punch the wall. Then, at the funeral service, he stood with his friend over to the side, just talking. And laughing.

That kind of ebb and flow of emotions is natural during dark times.

Don't try to cheer people up. Just ride the waves of emotion with them.

If they are sad when you are with them, let them be sad. If they are happy don't try to talk them out of that, either!

5. Praising people in Phase Three for 'being strong' or 'moving on'

Sometimes at a funeral, the family isn't crying and seems to be doing better than expected. We can be tempted to think that means they are really strong. We can make mini-heroes out of them.

I can tell you as someone who has often been behind the scenes in situations like this—many times they are medicated so they can make it through a few of the worst days of their life. If not, the adrenaline of the experience of being the family at a funeral can gloss over some of the deeper feelings they face when the crowds are gone.

What do we communicate when we praise people for being strong (i.e., not crying uncontrollably at the funeral)? We are telling them that this is a more appropriate or admirable way to respond when someone dies.

Which it isn't.

If I die tomorrow, I hope my kids, wife, family, and friends cry uncontrollably at least once or twice!

Not long ago one of my teenage sons was at a party when another boy accidentally pushed a piece of furniture into his bare foot. The result was that the nail on his big toe lifted like a trunk lid, and there was blood everywhere.

When I arrived at the house he was still crying.

And that's what he should have been doing. He was in pain, and he deserved to cry.

It's the same with people in emotional pain. It's okay for them to cry and not be strong. And when we praise them for being strong and moving on, we are saying, "That's the preferable response. If you are sad or depressed that is less desirable. It's more convenient for me if you are less sad because I am not confronted with as much pain when I think about you."

Praising people in Phase Three for moving on or being strong is a natural inclination, but it's not helpful.

For a practical tool to help you avoid these dangerous inclinations and know what to say when you visit the hospital, go to PatrickRiecke.com/resources. There

Phase Three

you will find a form to request a FREE wallet card telling you what to ALWAYS, SOMETIMES, and NEVER do when you visit a hospital.

Waiting for a Miracle, Playing God, and Advance Care Planning

Ed is a very elderly man whose family you have known for a long time. He has been sick for as long as you have known him, and you have visited him in the hospital many times. He is well-loved by his large family.

Now, Ed is hospitalized again. He is in respiratory failure, his kidneys are shutting down, and he has recently discovered an inoperable cancer mass. He is unresponsive; not doing well at all. You happen to be in the room when the physician comes to visit. She isn't very hopeful. Ed, she tells the family, is at the end of his life.

Planning While Hoping

You could tell that the tone of the family was negative before the doctor came in, but the situation escalates during the conversation.

As soon as the physician starts to sound like she's 'giving up', the tone of the family goes from tense to angry. And when she uses the phrase "Do not resuscitate" the family abruptly ends the conversation and tells her to get out in a way that seems to not only close the door to her, but to the entire idea that Ed might not overcome his current condition.

After the physician gracefully exits, the family turns to one another and you, and says things like, "Can you believe she wants us to pull the plug on dad/grandpa? She must not have any faith. We know he will get better."

You look at the motionless Ed, who has tubes coming and going everywhere, including a large tube that is in his mouth, helping him breathe. You certainly want to be optimistic, but things don't look good.

HOW TO TALK

A couple of days later you hear that Ed is still not getting any better, that the hospital still wants to take him off of his ventilator, but that Ed is still a full code[1] and is getting dialysis every few days.

Some questions that may arise from the family at this stage are listed below. Imagine the family asking you these questions.

Don't the doctors have any faith?

Shouldn't we do everything to save him?

Can't God heal him?

Shouldn't we at least keep him alive until Aunt Betty arrives from Arizona?

Should we look for an LTAC facility?[2]

Are we playing God if we take him off the vent?

PLAYING GOD

Let's pause for a moment on that last question. The others will come up in the rest of Ed's story, later.

---

1. Meaning that if his heart stops, he will have CPR and other interventions to bring his heartbeat back.
2. Long Term Acute Care Facility. These facilities can take care of patients like Ed for a longer time than hospitals.

Planning While Hoping

This question about playing God comes up surprisingly often.

Some people feel as though they are playing God if they remove medical interventions from their loved ones and that removal results in their death. And you can understand why they might feel that way. But another question naturally follows: *Were we playing God when we put the patient on the interventions?*

Some people equate God with what is natural. If you have ever been in the room of a patient who is near the end of life and she is connected to machines that are keeping her from dying right at that moment, you probably would not use the word 'natural' to describe the situation.

At one point, in healthcare, when the mechanical ventilation was removed from a patient, it was called a *terminal wean*. The meaning, of course, was clear: the patient was going to be weaned off the machines, and they were going to die.

The only problem with that phrase (although it is still used quite a lot) is that not all people die when they are weaned from the vent. Of course, some patients just needed help breathing for a shorter time and no one expected them to die when the vent was removed. But sometimes even when everyone *does* expect the patient to die, he doesn't.

So, the phrase *terminal wean* isn't always accurate.

Therefore, there has been a move among some healthcare workers to call this process a *vent withdrawal*.

This is a more descriptive phrase. There is a vent (the tube in the person's throat that is helping them breathe) that is being withdrawn. However, few people like to discuss withdrawing medical care that will result in the death of their loved one. Similarly, many times clinicians discuss "withdrawing care" or support. But that ignores the reality that even if all the machines are turned off, the team will still care for and care about the patient and family.

Recently, a new phrase has been introduced. Whether or not it will catch on is yet to be seen. But the new phrase is a positive change. Plus, it forms a nice acronym.

Allowing Natural Death. AND.

Our Bodies are trying to die [handwritten]

Planning While Hoping

This means we are going to get our medical interventions (ventilation, certain medications, etc.) out of the way and see what naturally occurs. While death is expected in many of these situations, it certainly won't occur in every situation.

But I have to say something about all this. Something that until now I have only said to my chaplains.

Sometimes our bodies are *trying* to die.

To oversimplify it significantly, perhaps it's helpful to think of when you are *trying* to sneeze. Your body feels the need to sneeze. It feels like it would be the most natural thing to do. It would be a relief to do it. But something has prevented you from sneezing.

In a much more profound way, sometimes our bodies as *trying* to die. And when an intervention is imposed to stop the dying process, that can be a miracle. Or it can leave the person feeling as though something artificial has happened that has left them somewhat frustrated.

Sometimes intervention for the patient whose body is trying to die is the right choice.

At other times, *allowing a natural death* is more appropriate.

ED'S WISHES: ADVANCE CARE PLANNING

There are other important questions for Ed. Questions that might take the focus off what the family wants, or what the healthcare team thinks is best, and shine a light on what Ed's wishes might be.

Did Ed previously express his wishes if he found himself in this situation? Did he ever have Advance Care Planning initiated? Does he have any advance directives completed?

What is an Advance Directive?

> Advance directive is a term that refers to your spoken and written instructions about your future medical care and treatment. By stating your healthcare choices in an advance directive, you help your family and physician understand your wishes about your medical care.[3]

If Ed completed an advance directive, it might answer questions such as:

---

3. https://www.in.gov/isdh/25880.htm

1. What does he want to be done medically?

Advance Care Planning covers important questions. It helps people consider (in advance) what medical interventions they might request or decline. This planning can answer questions about whether or not a patient would want to be on a ventilator for a long time, or how they would feel about having a medical situation that limited their ability to interact or understand the world around them

2. How far does he want to take his healthcare?

In an Advance Care Planning conversation, Ed may have indicated a preference concerning CPR or certain medicines or procedures in certain situations. That would certainly help the conversation between his family and the healthcare team.

3. Does Ed want to be intubated for a long time? Does he want a feeding tube?

Unfortunately, Ed is very sick. The standard, generally, is to only keep a patient intubated (the ventilator tube down their throat) for about two weeks. Since Ed isn't improving, the possibility of removing the ventilator means he might not survive. Did Ed ever indicate what he would want in this situation?

One of the most difficult conversations can center around the feeding tube. No one wants to think that they are starving their loved ones. But in some situations, a feeding tube may not be making the person better, and could even be a burden to the patient (failed tubes, infection, digestive concerns).

4. Did Ed think about nursing facilities?
Opinions about being in a long term care facility (nursing home, assisted living, etc.) vary widely. Some people embrace it as their new community. Others would rather die at home or in a hospital. Advance Care Planning helps a person think through these decisions before they become urgent.

5. What matters most to Ed as his health declines?
This is probably the most important question. Advance Care Planning facilitators are often trained to ask the question, "What does living well mean to you?" Or, "If you were having a good day, what would you be doing, what would be happening?" Answers vary from time spent with family, to going to work, to just being able to wake up and see the sunshine. But you can see how this question, answered in advance, would have helped Ed.

6. Who does Ed want to make his decisions?

Of course, Ed would like to make his own decisions about his healthcare. But right now, he cannot. He has a lot of family members who may have a variety of opinions. But is there one person in Ed's life that has talked with him about healthcare questions? And does that person have the courage to follow through on whatever his wishes may be? This designation of a health care representative, or health care agent, is not a difficult process. Our chaplains help patients complete these forms every day. They could have helped Ed complete one before he was quite so sick. If he hasn't done it by now, however, it may be too late.

7. Does Ed have any of this in writing?

This can be the most practical question. Having a difficult conversation about all these questions is the starting point. But having advance directive documents make healthcare decisions simpler.

A leading resource for having conversations that include such important questions is an organization called Respecting Choices®.[4] Also, your local state or federal government likely has some resources available.

Here are some basics for an advance directive form:

- The form must indicate the wishes of the patient.
- The form must be signed by the patient (meaning they must be able to understand what they are signing).
- The form must be signed by other witnesses or a notary, as required by the form or applicable local statutes.

8. What is the best-case scenario if we continue aggressive care?

Some people respond well to aggressive care. If the person is young, otherwise healthy, strong, has lots of support, these can all be factors that will help a person to have a positive outcome even if their current health situation is really scary.

---

4. https://respectingchoices.org/

Although Ed has lots of support, he is not young, strong, or otherwise healthy. Even if every medical intervention works perfectly, in what shape will it leave Ed?

9. How do you think Ed feels about his situation now, even though he is unresponsive and cannot tell us?

Even the least responsive patient will occasionally wince in pain. Or they might seem at peace. Or perhaps they are communicating non-verbally; a squeeze of a hand or nodding of the head, tears in the eyes, or other means. Even though Ed can't say much, we can learn a lot about how he is feeling about the situation based upon careful observation.

Is dialysis 'harming' if he is not going to recover? Dialysis can be a painful and involved process. There are needle sticks, flushing of fluids, rotating of the patient, and repeated tests. Having a tube in your throat to help you breathe is no different. Many patients who recover after being intubated report jaw soreness, a sensitive throat, and a dry cough for some time.

10. What will it look like if a Full Code is called for Ed?

A code is a violent event.

Chest compressions, shock to the chest, artificial respiration, and loads of medication are no small experience. It's not like in the movies where a few seconds of chest compressions and the person revives, sits up, and thanks his rescuer.

In fact, according to the American Heart Association, the statistics for CPR after cardiac arrest are not promising, even if the patient is in the hospital already.[5] In 2016, for example, less than 25% of patients who received CPR while hospitalized survived until their discharge from the hospital. Other reports show even lower success rates.

While every situation is unique, it's clear that being coded (receiving full interventional care if you lose your pulse) while in the hospital is not a good sign for your survival.

---

5. http://cpr.heart.org/AHAECC/CPRAndECC/General/UCM_477263_Cardiac-Arrest-Statistics.jsp

Planning While Hoping

To learn more about Advance Care Planning and many other topics, loaded with extra links and free resources, check out my YouTube channel by searching Patrick and Kristen Riecke.

+++

Some people want everything done in every situation, but many do not. My wife and I recently had an Advance Care Planning conversation, even though we are both healthy and young. Without revealing all of our wishes, I can confidently say that neither of us would want to be in Ed's situation.

If you would like to have an Advance Care Planning conversation, contact your physician, local hospital, or look for the appropriate documents on your local government website. For other introductions, simply search Advanced Care Planning. Lots of great tools are available online.

+++

Ed has multiple co-morbidities (diseases or illnesses that could cost him his life). He has respiratory failure (which is why he is on a breathing machine), his kidneys are shutting down, and he has significant cancer for which there is no real treatment.

If Ed has CPR, what are the chances that he will be the one in four who survives until he is discharged from the hospital?

But Ed's family insists that he will get better. They don't trust the hospital or anyone who tells them otherwise.

WAITING FOR A MIRACLE

Many times I have heard people talk about waiting for a miracle for their loved one. The idea that our mom, son, or grandpa might not make it out of this situation alive is so difficult to consider that our minds naturally want to escape. Sometimes, for people of faith, we can get stuck in Phase Two. Remember, the theme in Phase Two is *God will help me to overcome my difficulties.*

I have painfully witnessed parents of children who were imminently dying still holding on to the slim possibility that God will do something dramatic just before their child dies to save them and restore them to health.

I admit that once when I attended the funeral of a young person who should not have died yet, I prayed for that person to miraculously resurrect even during the funeral service itself! I was stuck in Phase Two.

Is there anything wrong with praying for a miracle?

No, of course not.

Let's put a finer point on it.

What are we doing when we pray for a miracle? The most accurate verb is *hope*. We are *hoping* that something will change. We place our faith in God, who can do whatever he would like at any point in time, and we *hope* that he will heal the sick person.

Hope helps the heart.

But hope is not a plan.

And sometimes, only focusing on that hope, talking about praying and hoping and not talking about preparing and processing can cause problems.

Think about Ed's family. Ed is a very sick, very elderly man. The medical team has served him well, and now it's their opinion that he is at the end of his life. And even if he does 'survive', they are painting a difficult picture of what life would look like for Ed. The family should expect a permanent ventilator, feeding tube, and twenty-four-hour care at least.

For Ed's family to continue to *only* hold out hope for his miraculous healing can raise many problems:

- **When we only hope for a miracle, we aren't dealing with the present.**

As I sat in one family meeting, the family members told the care team that they didn't want to hear anything negative because God was going to heal their sister. Meanwhile, their sister was so near death that it would certainly have taken a miracle to save her.

As a chaplain, they implored me to maintain hope that God would heal her. I told them I always maintain that hope for every sick patient who wishes to get better, but that we had to think about what we were going to do while we waited for a miracle.

By focusing only on hope for the future, they weren't able to deal with the present.

- **When we only hope for a miracle, and then the person dies, the pain is**

Planning While Hoping

multiplied.

After presenting the content of this book in a daylong workshop, one of the attendees came up to me and mentioned this topic of *waiting for a miracle*.

She was angry.

But not angry at me. She was angry at a recent family situation.

Her brother-in-law had died far too young.

He had children, her nieces, and nephews, at home and they were all devastated when he died.

But the devastation was made more complicated because of the presence of a faith community in the life of the family. The community was certain that the man would be healed, even until the very end. And whenever the family would seem to 'lack faith', the people from the church would scold them and tell them that God was going to do a miracle.

Whether or not God did a miracle, I do not know. But she told me that her brother-in-law had died and now the family is in shambles. Not only have they broken ties with that church (which is a good thing, in my opinion), they have gone their separate ways as a family (usually not a good thing). Some of the children have become substance abusers, others have been incarcerated. And none of them want to have anything to do with God or faith because God "let them down" so significantly.

Their dad's death would have been painful no matter what. But the heavy influence of a faith community that was stuck in Phase Two has multiplied their pain.

- **When we only hope for a miracle, we are usually telling God what qualifies as a miracle.**

Why I wonder, do we only describe the healing of a sick person as a miracle? Why can't I look at the sunrise and say it is miraculous? Or at the face of my child and say the same thing? The truth is, I do feel this way—every day is full of inspiration and divine goodness, in my opinion.[6]

But even for me, I recently described the physical recovery of a hospitalized loved one as "pretty miraculous."

---

6. That's why my social media presence is under the name "Routine Revelation".

Planning While Hoping

One day a chaplain was visiting a patient who was near the end of his life. During their conversation, the patient mentioned a son that he had not talked with in months. Something had happened, and they had a falling out. The hospitalized man was confident that his son would not be coming to see him.

Probing just a bit, our chaplain asked, "Would you like it if he did come to see you?"

The man paused and was silent for a long time. That's not unusual for someone in the hospital. Between the pain, the sickness, and medication, sometimes we need to wait patiently.

Our chaplain finished the story with tears in his own eyes. "As I sat there watching his face, I saw one tear roll down. Then another. Then I noticed that his phone was in his hands. He was staring at the phone. I could guess what he was thinking. Finally, he looked up at me through many tears and said. 'Yes. Yes, I would like it if he would come to see me.'"

Before the chaplain could exit the room this patient was on the phone with his son.

Friends, that is miraculous.

When I sat in the funeral service for that young person and prayed for her to miraculously come back to life, that was understandable. But the real miracle is the beauty and healing and meaning that came later, once she was gone.

Remember, we can *always* hope for a miracle.

But we must not *only* hope for a miracle.

And we must never limit what kind of miracle we would accept.

Doing robust Advance Care Planning is a gift not only to those you love but to yourself as well.

Planning (while hoping) is always appropriate.

Ch. 9

Faith Vs. Medicine: Dignify the Dying Person

[Handwritten notes:
Ed
God vs the Doctors
Bethany – Stage 3
"I know I am going to die" — write letter
"I like to write" — Record video]

You visit Ed in the hospital again a few days later. Only a few family members are at his bedside as the early morning sunlight shoots through the room. The sunlight contrasts with the dark sadness of the family, and the clinical beeping of that hovers over Ed.

Ed is stuck.

He did not do any Advance Care Planning. He has no advance directives completed.

It seems he never said much about what he would want to be done in a situation like this.

And it seems no one asked.

Now his condition is static—the machines are keeping him from dying, but they aren't making him better. His family continues their 'do everything and wait for a miracle' approach. Likely, because of this, the family and the care team are no longer enjoying good communication. Every time his nurse comes in, she seems tense and defensive, and the family seems dismissive of her. You get the feeling that the doctors have been avoiding Ed's room when the family is visiting.

When there is a breakdown between the patient, family, and healthcare team, there are no winners.

GOD VS. THE DOCTORS

In chapter five, we discovered some of the natural, but dangerous, inclinations when Phase Three is approaching. Another practice seems helpful, but can be hurtful to the family and patient.

Sometimes people can portray medical situations as 'God vs. the Doctors.'

Sometimes, people of faith can feel at odds with the clinical team. They may say things like:

"The doctors don't have the final word."

"God will decide when I am going to die, not the doctors."

"People all over the planet are praying for my dad. I know that prognosis can't be true."

While these feelings can be genuine, they can lead to a dangerous dichotomy. For a long time, some people have felt a tension between faith and medicine—religion and science. It can seem as if it's some kind of competition where only one (the doctor or God) can win.

But when we are gathered around a hospital bed, painting the situation as God vs. the Doctors doesn't help anyone.

I've met some people who think that most physicians are anti-faith or even atheists. Of course, that's not true. A 2005 study discovered that doctors in the United States are people of faith at a rate that is nearly identical to the rest of the population.[1] My suspicion is that's also the case in most other countries.

When a doctor tells you that he or she thinks you are going to die—they hope they are wrong, too.

1. http://www.foxnews.com/story/2005/06/23/most-us-doctors-believe-in-god-study-says.html

Doctors don't wish for patients to die.

Quite the contrary.

The greatest fear for many physicians is the death of a patient. Dr. Atul Gawande is quite vulnerable on this point in his book, *Being Mortal*. Physicians usually err on the side of doing too much to save a person's life and being too optimistic, not the other way around. Estimates of patient survival given by physicians ("you have six months to live") are usually heavily influenced by the optimism of the physician.

In one study, researchers discovered that while the physicians' prediction of survival (of cancer patients) averaged 42 days, *actual* survival averaged only 29 days.[2] That means that the physicians were holding out *more* hope than warranted, not less.

Many believe this overestimation of survival is the result of the emotional struggle many physicians feel when discussing patients' prognosis with them. Imagine having to be the person who comes into a room and tells a family that their loved one is going to die in less than a year or less than a month. Naturally, physicians shy away from this harsh reality.

2. https://www.ncbi.nlm.nih.gov/pubmed/12881260

The point is this—no matter the faith, the people skills, the tone, the education, or anything else—the doctor wants the best possible outcome for every patient in every situation. They are hard-wired to want this so much that they usually cannot bring themselves to admit how long (or short) they think you will live.

It does not help anyone to paint the situation as God vs. the Doctors. If I am a patient in a hospital bed with a scary diagnosis or injury, I need to feel that everyone is on my side—my family, my faith community, *and* my clinical care team.

Patients, friends, family, people from the faith community, can certainly have an important dialogue with the healthcare team. But should be careful not to describe the situation as a competition between God and the care team.

BETHANY

At first, your young friend, Bethany, struggled.

Surgery, radiation, then chemotherapy.

Her cancer was aggressive, but as her dad said, she is a fighter. The prayers were flying up to heaven. The church rallied around the family, bringing meals, sending notes, watching the kids, and checking in with the family. After all her treatments, Bethany was much weaker, but she was said to be in remission.

Several months later, however, Bethany's dad called you again.

"The cancer is back," he said. Treatments began right away. At the end of that round of treatments, though still treating her aggressively, the doctors gave her a less optimistic outlook.

That's when your phone rings again.

This time it's Bethany.

Although her voice is thin, her spirit is strong. She asks if she can meet with you. You rearrange your schedule for that very afternoon.

When Bethany sits down across from you, you remember her as a young girl in your church. She has always been full of life, and a joy to her parents, friends, and others at the church. You remember one year when she had the lead role in a children's play. She sang a sweet little song that brought you to tears.

You remember her very much at Phase One of her spiritual life—accepting the news that God loves her and has a wonderful plan for her life.

You think of her dad and mom.

Although many people seem to primarily sympathize with Bethany herself or Brad or the kids, you keep thinking about Bethany's parents. You have always had so much respect for them, and they have always seemed like such strong people.

Bethany's sickness has broken their hearts.

You can't help but put yourself in their shoes and think about how it must feel as you helplessly watch your daughter, the mother of your precious grandchildren, face such a significant struggle. They are in Phase Two—asking God to help them overcome their difficulties.

As Bethany sits down across from you, you realize that it might be the first time you have talked with her by herself, without the rest of the crowd around. Her gaze is serious and piercing. Her body may have changed, but her engaging presence has only become more focused.

HOW TO TALK

The conversation is different this time.

Bethany has arrived in Phase Three.

You swallow hard, sensing what is coming.

After brief small talk, Bethany sits up straight in her seat.

"I know I am going to die."

She says as she sips a warm coffee and peers over the edge of the cup. The look on her face isn't tentative, but she seems to be allowing you a moment to hear what she has just said.

"I know my three kids are going to lose their mom before any of them reach adulthood." Small tears form in the corners of her eyes. "I am sad for Haley and Micah. They will remember me, and I generally think that's a good thing. But Emma won't even remember me, at least not like Haley and Micah. Sometimes, that keeps me up at night."

Now you take a sip of your drink, hoping it can warm your hands and face because they have gone cold. Bethany pauses, gathers her strength after the pain that surfaced when she said Emma's name.

She continues.

"I know Brad is going to be a widower before he even reaches middle age. He's been so supportive, and now…" Her voice trails, and so does her gaze.

Then she says the phrase that brings tears to your eyes. "My parents."

Their faces come into your mind.

You both pick up napkins from the table to curb your sniffles.

"I had a dream last night that they were standing at the front of the church. They were both crying. My dad's arm was around my mom. They were dressed like it was Sunday morning, but it wasn't."

Her large brown eyes brim again as she puts her hands on the table, her fingers on the tabletop, and her thumb under it. Like she is steadying herself. She looks at you and says, "They were standing in front of my casket."

Her tears tumble.

Your tears tumble.

You both wipe your eyes and simply wait for the moment to be complete.

Later, you won't be sure how you thought to ask this next question, but it bubbles up out of you.

"What do you want to do?" you ask, hoping that's not the stupidest thing someone could say at this moment.

Bethany does not look at you. She looks at her hands in her lap. You can tell she is deep in thought and she seems to be rallying supernatural courage. Cancer may have taken most of her physical strength, but her inner strength seems to have only grown.

After what seems like a long time, her head stays down, but her eyes turn up to you.

"I like to write." She almost grins with the anticipation of what she is about to do.

"Could I…" she probes you to see if you think she is crazy.

"Could I write letters to people and then give them to you to hold on to until…" You know that she means until she dies, but you won't make her say it out loud.

A couple of tears bubble up again, but they are not altogether sad this time. There is a little bit of excitement mixed in this time as you nod your head while she tells you the rest of her plan.

PHASE THREE

In this meeting with Bethany, we have had a distilled experience in Phase Three. Before we go on to the next chapter for our friend Margaret, let's pause to honor what has just happened with Bethany.

Phase Three: When God brings meaning out of suffering

Something beautiful is happening at this moment while Bethany talks with you. Her letters have a good chance to change the lives of those who receive them. What she is doing is important work—it's sacred.

So, two questions to consider before we move on:

What if you, as her friend, family member, or faith leader had tried to stay in PhaseTwo—trying to overcome?

You could have discouraged her from giving up. You could have told her that God could still heal her. You could have told her to stay positive. You could have asked her about the next, more aggressive treatment that the doctors have made available.

There is certainly a time to do all of that. But the question is—does Bethany feel like it's time to have this conversation? Remember what she said when she sat down?

"I know I am going to die."

She wasn't being morbid. She had thought already about the implications of her death—how it would impact her husband, kids, and her parents. She had thought this through. Therefore, she needed you to go to that phase with her, not to try to force her into a different phase. If you had just kept telling her that she would overcome, when she has realized that's not likely, you could have lost her trust.

What if you had tried theology or defending God or focusing on the afterlife?

You could have told her that God is all-powerful and he is the Great Physician. True. You could have told her that God has the final word, not the doctors. That's also true. Or, accepting that she was going to die, you could have told her that there was nothing to be afraid of because she would be in heaven, where all her pain would be over. That may be true as well.

But today, Bethany has to leave your coffee meeting and go home and look in the eyes of a toddler who doesn't know that her mom won't be there when she graduates from Kindergarten. The hope of heaven is real for many people but doesn't always help at a time like this.

As far as trusting God as the Great Physician, that's what Bethany has been trying to do since she was first diagnosed. Chances are she has trusted God with her medical status more than most people. Life has required it of her.

But, because you waded into Phase Three with her and simply asked her, "What do you want to do?" significant meaning is being brought out of her great suffering. Maybe when you asked her that question, you had to swallow hard. Maybe you felt like she was giving up. Maybe you felt like *you* were giving up. Maybe you felt like you were letting her parents down by even accepting that the outcome for Bethany might not be physical healing. Stepping into Phase Three can be scary, but it can also be liberating. Father Richard Rohr observed about these Phase

Three moments. "Suffering seems to overcome the semi-permeable membrane between ourselves, others and God—and sometimes rather completely."[3]

In our last chapter before a postscript, we will revisit all of our friends—Ed, Margaret, and Bethany—as well as their friends and family. We already know that Bethany is in Phase Three. And although Ed's family can't accept it, his desperate medical situation means Ed has arrived in Phase Three, as well. Can meaning still be brought out of his suffering? What about Margaret and her grandson, Eli?

3. Eager to Love, p.26

How to Talk with a Grieving Person

There are clichés we often hear when it comes to grief. However, many of them are short-sighted, unhelpful, and hurtful. In this chapter, let's consider eight clichés that might be doing more harm than good when we talk with people in grief. Following what NOT to say, I'll give you some alternatives that will be more helpful.

What NOT to Say

Before you read this list and think "Oh no, I'm a terrible person. I've said these things before," just stop. We have all said these things. That is what makes them cliché. I've said them, you've said them, and they usher forth from a pure heart and good intentions. So, don't dump guilt on yourself. Rather, let them open your eyes a bit more to what it's like to be in grief.

1. Everything happens for a reason

What's the reason? If my wife just died, what logical reason will be sufficient to help me accept that she is, suddenly, gone forever? Even when really amazing things happen following a death, those blessings don't provide a good enough *reason* for my loved one to be gone from this world.

I have several friends who have established nonprofit organizations to bless others following the death of their children. That has prompted many well-meaning people to say this cliché to them. However, each one of them would trade away their nonprofit to have Kate or Rowan or Erin back in their lives. They are grateful that the ministry or organization came about after their child's death, but it does not give a good *reason* for their death.

Kate Bowler, in the wake of her stage four cancer diagnosis, provides a beautiful and poignant book entitled *Everything Happens for a Reason: And Other Lies I've Loved*. Please make that the very next book you read. It will make you laugh and cry and realize that some common clichés we utter need to be reconsidered.

2. God needed another angel in heaven

First of all, there isn't any evidence in the Hebrew or Christian scriptures that this actually happens. People don't become angels. And being an angel isn't better than being a person. Being a human being is the best it gets unless you are God. Besides that, while the image of a placid-faced winged cherub invisibly fluttering around you with the spirit of your dead loved one is comforting to some, it is not comforting to all.

Finally, what kind of God *needs* to kill people, or let them die?

3. You need to move on, it's been...

Elisabeth Kübler-Ross in 1969 published her book *On Death and Dying*. Out of that book came the famous "five stages of grief". Kübler-Ross never intended to portray grief as a straight line from denial (the first stage) to acceptance (the fifth stage). However, she has been interpreted in this way. The result? People think that you must move through the stages sequentially, never doubling back, and always moving forward until you are... *done*.

Recent experts on grief have taken serious issue with the notion of linear movement through a "grief process". Instead of a straight line from stage one to stage five, grief is more adequately understood like a toddler's scribble. The line switches back on itself, covers territory many times, takes sharp turns with no warning, and never ends. Therefore, please never suggest that a grieving person should *move on* after a certain amount of time.

4. Time heals all wounds

This is the kinder counterpart to the previous cliché. The problem with this one is that it almost sounds right. But consider this. Do you know anyone that you might describe as "stuck" in grief that happened a long time ago, maybe even decades? If so, has time healed all wounds? No.

It is certainly true that time can change the complexion of grief, but time does not heal all wounds. In fact, grief can suddenly pop up many years later as fresh as it was at first.

5. God must have needed them more than you do

This one has similar problems to "God needed another angel in heaven". It cuts in two ways. It paints God as selfish during a season when the griever needs God to be caring. Second, it minimizes their connection with their loved one.

6. At least…

Kate Bowler calls this "brightsiding". It comes in many forms.

At least you got to say goodbye.
At least you had a lot of years together.
A least you didn't have time to get attached.
At least you know where she's going.
At least it was quick.
At least you had a long time to prepare.
At least you still have other living children.

This cliché, like others, does two hurtful things. First, it minimizes the grief of the griever. Any statement that begins with *at least* puts two realities on a scale. On one side is their loss. On the other side is whatever reality with which the *at least* statement concludes (e.g., other living children, many years, the promise of heaven, etc.). The implication is that there are realities that could *outweigh* their grief. However, if you have ever carried real grief, you know this isn't true. Second, *at least* comments are trying to *fix* a situation that cannot be fixed. After all, if I can convince you that the promise of heaven is greater than the pain of grief, you'll stop being so sad and I'll feel like I solved your problem.

7. Trust God

Similarly to what we discussed in the chapter on how to visit the hospital, never doubt the faith of a grieving person. Would it be good if they could trust God? Of course. Perhaps they are trusting God more in their grief than they ever have. *Telling* them they need to trust God sounds like *scolding*. As a general rule, never scold a person's faith if they are facing more difficult circumstances than you are facing.

8. Let me know what you need/How can I help?

I admit I still let this cliché tumble out of my heart occasionally. It feels so altruistic and helpful. After all, we want to help in a way that makes sense to the *griever,* not just to us. But there is a problem with that. When you are in grief it is very hard to know what you need. Even harder to ask for what you need.

Grief is disorienting. If you use this cliché, the person might think "Oh great, not only is it my job to grieve well, now I also have to figure out how you can help me, too." That's why this open-ended and well-meaning cliché can actually be counterproductive.

Instead, try one of these:

> "I'd like to bring dinner over Tuesday. Are there any dietary restrictions I should be aware of?"
>
> "When I mow my grass next time, I'm just going to come over and mow yours, too."
>
> "I'm going to call you Thursday after lunch, just to see how you are doing. If you don't want to talk, I understand. If you do, I'll make sure I have lots of time."

What TO Say

Don't feel guilty if you have said many of the things on the list above. They are called clichés because they are said often. Most of them come from a pure heart that wants to help. Next, let's look at some phrases *to* say to a person in grief. These aren't catchy like the clichés, so you may have to stop after each one and say it out loud to yourself. We need practice to get these phrases into our vocabulary.

1. I'm sorry Stephen died

This short statement has three positives. First, it acknowledges what happened. It wasn't just a "loss" or "hard time". Someone died. And nothing compares to that.

Second, this phrase names the deceased. When a person dies, their name vacates our vocabulary. Never again will we say, "Stephen called yesterday", or "I'm making dinner when Stephen gets home", or "Stephen, can you please take your laundry upstairs." Because of this, people who loved Stephen feel an ache. Their hearts can *feel* the discontinued use of his name. When you say it out loud in this phrase, *I'm sorry Stephen died*, you honor his life.

Third, this phrase communicates that you are also sad this happened. Not in the same way as those closest to him, but in a parallel way. It communicates that you wish he hadn't died. That wish is at the core of their experience of grief, and they will appreciate hearing you identify it.

2. I don't fully understand, but I think God does

It was several days later that I finally had this realization in my own life. My wife, Kristen, and I experienced a second-trimester miscarriage. It devastated us as a young couple. My son's death was certainly the worst thing that had happened to us at that point in our lives. I was a ministry intern at the time. I preached and taught regularly. But it still took days before this thought occurred to me. "God's son also died."

For those who believe that Jesus is the son of God the Father, we must believe that God the Father felt grief when Jesus died a violent and untimely death. I found that strangely comforting. While few others could even come close to understanding my sadness, God could. God, I would argue, has more experience with grief than any expert whose books we devour. While grief responses to faith vary widely, it can only help to view God as compassionate and understanding.

3. This feels wrong because it is wrong

We were created for life. We were created for connection. We were not created to die. It is a natural part of life, but it still feels like such a violation. This sense of *wrongness* is amplified if the person dies at a young age, and multiplied in the case of a child or baby. Kristen often says, "I'm not supposed to hold the hand of my child when he dies. He's supposed to hold my hand." People often die *out of order*. All death represents a separation, which is a violation of our nature. When death comes too soon, tragedy also feels like a travesty.

4. What you are feeling is normal

Kristen and I led a live online event this week around the topic of miscarriage and stillbirth. I asked participants to type in the chat emotions that a mom might feel when she loses a baby. They listed emotions like:

- Sadness
- Embarassment
- Confusion
- Anger
- Guilt
- Lostness
- Envy
- Unbelief
- "It's not fair" and

- Gratitude

All of those feelings are normal. We can affirm all those feelings in a grieving person. No feeling should be considered *wrong* or discouraged. It might make *me* more comfortable if the person is sad than if they are angry; grateful instead of envious. But it's not about me. If the person is feeling anything short of suicidal (a different topic altogether), we can affirm those feelings as normal. Do NOT try to talk them out of their feelings.

5. This person will always be a part of your life

The cliché "They will live on with you in your heart" isn't exactly what I mean. I don't think that cliché is necessarily hurtful. That's why I didn't list it in what NOT to say. But I mean something more basic. The deceased impacted the griever in some way. They shaped their life either a little or a lot. Because of that, that person doesn't suddenly cease to exist when they die. They *do* live on. They live on through their influence and through their absence.

In our book, *No Matter How Small*, we tell the story of Jayda and Toby. Toby struggled after Jayda experienced a miscarriage. He found it strange that he still felt so attached to his daughter. Even though he never held her in his arms, he felt her absence in a tangible way. Toby thought it was unnatural to feel so attached to someone who was gone. Fortunately, an insightful counselor showed him that attachment to your daughter, dead or alive, is the most natural feeling in the world. Those who have died will *always* remain a part of our lives.

6. I'm with you

Grief can be isolating. Telling a griever that you are with them and you will *continue* to be with them in the days ahead can remove that sense of isolation.

7. You have options

Burial, cremation, funeral, memorial service, graveside, etc. These options can feel overwhelming in the days after a person dies. Decision fatigue can set in quickly. After the funeral, options can seem to disappear. Giving the griever options can help them interact with their grief in a healthier way.

Here are five categories:

Events like community memorial services are sometimes put on by community groups (hospitals, places of worship, counseling centers, etc.). These events have two significant benefits. First, they usually come months after the griever's loved one died. That means that this option will affect them in a different way than the funeral. Whatever services are chosen immediately after death, those closest to the person might be in a fog. Those initial events might seem surreal and later be remembered as a blur. Attending some kind of memorial service further down the road can both honor the fact that they still miss that person *and* give them the opportunity to express their grief with a clearer mind. Second, events like these give them the chance to grieve alongside others. Seeing that there are others (maybe total strangers) who are in grief as well can be a solace. These events can be good options for the person in grief.

Tokens of remembrance may be treasured for years to come. Gifts like these could include wind chimes, a picture frame, a key chain, an engraved stone, a holiday ornament or candle, or even stickers for an automobile. These tokens provide a purposeful way to think about their loved ones. Consider the gift carefully, though. Will this be a happy remembrance for years? Is there a cliché engraved that might not always be helpful? Does the greiver seem like they appreciate this kind of gift?

Words to the deceased could be expressed in a handwritten letter, typed note, or written on the side of a balloon released to the sky. Other options of speaking to your deceased loved one include writing words on a paper that is then burned, a letter in a bottle sent out to sea, or tracing words with your toe on a sandy shore. Many of us wish we could still talk with our loved ones. Choosing one of these options helps to heal our hearts.

Anniversaries and birthdays present options for remembering those who have died. If you are supporting a person in grief, record the person's birthday as well as the day they died in your calendar. In the years ahead, contact the griever on those special days to let them know you are thinking about them. In the same way, you can encourage the person in grief to plan to embrace these annual days instead of simply dreading them.

Holidays also present their own opportunities. While most people dread the first year full of holidays, we also have the option to purposefully remember the person who has died. A friend of ours often tells her story of how she used a family get-together as a way to remember her stillborn daughter, Nora. She simply placed a candle on the table and lit it. "This represents Nora. She's not here, and we wish she was."

8. I have time

If you are supporting a person in grief, they might be scared to burden you with their thoughts and feelings. I didn't do it on purpose, necessarily, but earlier this week I told three people in one day that if they wanted to talk that I had time. One was saying goodbye to his mother in an ICU room. Another was in a surgery waiting area for his spouse. And the third was just having a down morning. One of the three took me up on the offer. When we talked on the phone later about another topic, I circled back around and asked how he was doing. Because I told him I had time, he shared more than he would have otherwise. Obviously, you have to mean it. You have to actually have time, or be willing to make the time. If you can't, that's ok. In that case, try, "This is really important. I really want to hear about how you are doing. Can we talk on Tuesday afternoon? I'll clear my schedule and make sure I give you all the time you need to talk about Stephen."

Some of the phrases in the first list of what NOT to say roll off the tongue more easily than the phrases in the second list. They are, after all, clichés. That means that we need to practice more helpful phrases. Please do that now. Go back to the second list and repeat them each out loud. Then do it again. Then do it again. These will become more natural for you as time goes on, and you will become more helpful to a grieving friend.

Finding Meaning in Suffering

MARGARET

Margaret is near retirement age. She has recently discovered that she has ALS, also known as Lou Gehrig's disease. It's a progressive and terminal disease. Initially, Margaret experienced diminished use of her hands. Now, however, some medication and therapy has helped her to live a normal life.

Margaret has some concerns as she comes to grips with her diagnosis. First, she is worried about caring for her grandson, Eli. Her daughter depends on her daily. And Eli is a joy. He's a bright-eyed four-year-old with whom Margaret has had a special connection since his birth. Eli still has nearly two years before he will go to school every day.

Margaret's daughter could not afford it if she had to pay a daycare service. Besides, no one can replace grandma.

She's also very used to being part of the weekly services at her place of worship. She asks if you think she should tell the pastor to take her off the schedule. After all, it may become more difficult for her to usher without drawing attention to her ALS.

Lastly, like many people with ALS, Margaret is worried about her breathing. She's been told that most people with ALS die when their ability to breathe finally fails. ALS affects the muscular system, which is needed to get a deep breath. Margaret is anxious when she thinks about this future possibility.

As Margaret's disease progressed, she had a couple of days when her daughter had to make other arrangements. Happily, though, Margaret was able to care for Eli for quite some time. It gave her great joy. Even when he went into school, she picked him up three days a week. His special 'grandma time,' as Eli called it. Their favorite spot to visit was a soft-serve ice cream shop. Margaret always got the low-sugar, fruity flavors, but not Eli. He piled gummy worms and sprinkles on his chocolate ice cream.

As happens for most ALS patients, Margaret's capabilities began to wane. Eventually, she could no longer drive. That's what broke her heart. Grandma time started to be hard to come by. But Eli and his mom visited often, even when Margaret needed to move into a nursing home. She could no longer get around the home she had lived in for the past twenty-five years. Margaret could no longer scoop Eli into her arms. Part of that was because he was growing like a weed. But he would still come and sit by his grandma and snuggle close.

Margaret had always ushered at her church. She and others would walk down at offering time, once the prayer requests had all been prayed over, and she would simply pass the offering plate. But handling the plate became difficult pretty quickly.

She told you, a faithful friend during her illness, that she was going to meet with the pastor. She planned to tell him that she was going to quit helping on the weekends. You understood, and it didn't seem like a big deal to you. But you could tell that it was a huge deal to Margaret. It seemed to symbolize her illness. She hated how ALS affected her dexterity, and this was a public way that her incapacity was beginning to show.

A few weeks later, you visited with Margaret.

"Did you meet with the Pastor?" You asked.

"I sure did," Margaret had an unexpected twinkle in her eye.

"Ok," you laughed a little. "And…?"

"I won't be passing the plate anymore. Just can't do it!" She seemed more pleased to say this than you expected. "I've been…" she paused briefly and raised her eyebrows very purposefully. ALS was making speech more difficult, but she compensated for that by being intentional about her words. "I've been *promoted*." You could tell she was teasing you and had something special to say.

"What do you mean, you've been promoted?" You asked.

"You'll see this Sunday." She grinned.

Sure enough, you had a small surprise on Sunday. When the ushers headed to the back, Margaret stood as well. Nothing was different, yet. But she did not go to the back of the sanctuary. She began walking, with a little difficulty, to the front.

The pastor, who usually led prayer time before offering, nodded at Margaret and sat down.

Margaret turned slowly on her heel.

"For what needs can our church be praying this morning?" Margaret asked.

After the service, you found Margaret right away. She was beaming. You knew she had always been a person who loved to pray. She told you how when she tried to tell the pastor that she couldn't help any more, she broke down in tears right there in his office chair.

"That's when Pastor said, 'Margaret dry your tears. God is not done with you yet.' He told me he knew that I love to pray. He invited me to take over the prayer time. Before I knew what I was doing, I said yes! I don't know how long I will be able to keep it up, but I am sure glad to be included. Who knows, maybe I can be a blessing to people even while I am starting to lose my grip on my health."

At first, it was a little uncomfortable when Margaret led the prayer time at church. Margaret wasn't used to speaking, and her ALS made her speech difficult to understand. But she stuck with it, and the pastor was gracious. People started to bypass him to ask Margaret for prayer directly. Eli had lots of friends at church, and he started bringing kids with problems to his grandma for prayer. Margaret was praying for everything from a sick Labrador puppy (belonging to Eli's friend, Sarah) to families grieving the loss of their loved ones.

One week, though, something amazing happened. Margaret was having more trouble than usual getting her words out because of the progression of her ALS. Heads started to un-bow, and eyes started to open as they looked up at the leader that they loved a little more every week. Tears started to flow down her cheeks as she changed her prayer focus.

She was angry.

She started to tell God how much she hated having ALS. How she just did not understand why he hadn't healed her. No one could remember exactly what she said after that, but Eli explained it this way…

"God understands, even when other people can't."

The next ten minutes of the service were spent with everyone encircling Margaret and hugging her.

That experience didn't stop her. And it certainly didn't stop people from asking her to pray for them. If anything, Margaret's 'angry prayer' made her even more popular. Now she was getting more requests for prayer than ever before. As her capacity to speak continued to wane, you and others started to feel that her unspoken connection to God was greater than anyone could imagine.

The first week that Margaret could not attend service due to her final hospitalization was hollow and sad. Her prayer-time presence could not be replaced when the pastor filled in for her.

+++

Margaret died late on a Saturday, surrounded by family. Her daughter called you just after you had gone to bed to give you the news.

Although you felt sad, you also felt a deep sense of gratitude.

Most other people from church heard the news of her death for the first time when the pastor announced it during prayer time the next morning.

Tears flowed.

HOW TO TALK

Eli's friend, Sarah, whose puppy was healed by now, cried the rest of the morning.

Eli did not cry at church. Maybe it was because he had cried plenty the night before, at Grandma's. After all, he was in her room at the nursing home when she died. His mom wasn't sure that was a good idea, but Eli would not take 'no' for an answer.

"I need just a little more 'grandma time'." He said.

At Margaret's funeral service, you were amazed at how many people recalled the week when she prayed her 'angry prayer'. And so many people asked her for prayer in the last few years, she will be sorely missed.

At the funeral, you overheard Eli tell several people, "Remember, even if other people can't understand you, God understands."[1]

---

1. If you ever have to perform a funeral or memorial service, I recommend my friend Dr. Jon Swanson's book, "Giving a Life Meaning". It's a great practical tool that will help you know what to do and say.

ED

Ed remained unresponsive and intubated while his family kept demanding that the doctors do everything to save him. He had never said anything about what he would want in this situation.

At first, they resisted allowing Ed to die so Aunt Betty could come from Arizona. Then they wanted him to be moved to a long-term facility where he could remain intubated. All the while, Ed was getting dialysis, remained a full code, and he was slowly going downhill.

On day 17 of Ed's hospitalization, at eleven-thirty at night, his heart failed

A code was called and CPR performed since that was still what the family wanted.

Ed, an elderly and frail man, received chest compressions, shock to his chest, and extreme medications.

Only three members of the large family were there when the Code Blue was called—Ed's youngest daughter and her two children. Ed's 17-year-old granddaughter, Tanisha, and his 14-year-old grandson, Brian, watched as a team of more than a dozen went to work on their papaw.

Ed died after being coded for 47 traumatic minutes.

His frail body nearly broke under CPR. All because his family got stuck in Phase Two.

All the tubes coming in and out of his body were askew, and he seemed to be in agony as he died in front of his grandchildren.

When we are willing to wade into Phase Three, beautiful things happen. People like Margaret pray in ways we could never have imagined. Meaning is found, like Bethany writing letters.

But when we try to stay in Phase One or Two, we can miss the meaning that's possible in suffering.

Ed's family missed a chance to find meaning in his suffering.

What if they could have entered Phase Three?

Maybe they would have stood around his bed, sharing their favorite stories of their father and grandfather. Maybe Brian, his youngest grandchild, would have learned that his grandfather always wanted to be a poet and that he had a box full of poetry at home. And maybe, just maybe, Brian would have taken those poems, typed them up, and put them in a book. And maybe Brian would have followed in his footsteps and done some co-writing with his grandpa's archived poems later in life, and published their work together. Instead, what did Brian get in the last moments of his grandpa's life?

A traumatic image of death, a distrust of healthcare, and maybe a loss of faith in God.

Since Brian was the only one in the family that would have been inclined to do all this with the poetry, and since the family never waded into Phase Three, Brian had no idea his grandpa was a poet. Those possibilities disappeared like a vapor of things that could have been.

That's why it's so important, when it's time, to walk with people into Phase Three when meaning needs to be brought out of suffering.[2]

---

2. If Ed's family had read my book "How to Find Meaning in Your Life Before it Ends", they would have found 101 ways to find meaning instead of just fighting while Ed was dying.

BETHANY

Bethany was right.

Seven weeks after your talk, Bethany died at home. Brad was lying in the bed next to her, holding her close and covering her with his tears. Their three children, including Emma, the toddler, slept in their beds. Bethany's mom and dad kept vigil in the family room.

After lots of hugs, calls, and preparations, Bethany's funeral service draws a large crowd.

You have nearly two dozen letters in a small box—all by the same author.

Although the box only weighs a couple of pounds, it feels heavy to you. Your friend's letters have lived with you for the last couple of weeks. You aren't sure if they have been haunting you or blessing you. But their presence in your home has been powerful.

On the way to the funeral, you carefully tuck the box under your arm. Each envelope has a single name handwritten on the outside. They are sealed, and you certainly have not seen what is inside any of them.

+++

"What's this?" Brad asks as you hand him a thick envelope with his name on it.

You hadn't even considered that he might ask this question.

Choking back a world of emotion, you touch the sleeve of Brad's charcoal suit coat and look into his eyes.

"It's from Bethany," you say before your chin starts to quiver.

Brad still looks young to you, and his weary face now goes white.

"Oh my God," is all he can say. You remember when he first held Haley in his arms fifteen years ago. Now, he holds Bethany's letter with a similar look of awe on his face.

Haley finishes a conversation with a friend and comes up beside her dad.

Looking at his expression, she asks what's going on.

"What's that?" she asks, looking at her dad's letter. "It looks like mom's handwriting. But it can't…"

When she turns to look at you, your outstretched hand holds another envelope. It's nearly as thick as her dad's.

On the top is scrawled the name 'Haley'.

Always the intuitive one of the children, she knows immediately what this is. She claps her hand over her mouth and sinks her head into your left shoulder.

Other envelopes have the names of her other two children—Micah and Emma. Micah just says, "cool" and stuffs it in his pocket. Emma will get hers when she is older. Bethany's mom and dad helped Bethany a bit, so they are not as surprised as others. Still, they realize how special this is.

"Thank you," says her dad. "You know, after she met with you a few months ago, she called me. She told me she was going to start doing this. At first, I wasn't too excited because I felt like it meant the end of her life was getting close. But, here we are."

He glances towards Bethany, in a simple white dress. She is thin, but lovely in her casket. He continues, "You helped her to give a gift to us that will live with us forever. Thank you for being willing to have that conversation with Bethany when we couldn't."

Bethany Was Right

He takes his wife by the hand, and they step over to Bethany, putting their hands on hers.

In a sudden flash, you remember your friends's dream of this very scene.

Bethany dreamed about seeing her parents at church, wearing Sunday clothes, standing at her casket. You realize it was that dream that prompted her to start writing letters. Time seems to stand still.

After handing out several other envelopes with similar reactions, the funeral service is underway when the pastor motions for you to come to the front.

One envelope is still in the box.

It has your name on it, but it's not only for you.

Bethany asked you not to read it until her funeral.[3] You pull it out of the box and stand to your feet.

You slowly, reverently, open the letter. Bethany had wonderful handwriting. Even as she grew weaker, it was still beautiful. You begin to read:

Friends,

---

3. For a great practical resource on funeral's, check out my friend Dr. Jon Swanson's book, *Giving a Life Meaning*.

When I was young, I always dreamed of having the life I had before I was diagnosed. I won't say that every day was perfect, but now I realize how fortunate I was—how fortunate I am. I believed in God's purposes for my life pretty easily. I could feel his love wrap around me like a warm blanket.

Even when I was first diagnosed, it seemed impossible that I would die from this cancer. After all, I was young and strong. How often I recalled the lessons I learned as a child. And for a long time, I simply knew God would help me get through this. I prayed every day that I would be healthy again. And I know that many of you prayed that prayer with me. So many people visited, called, wrote notes, brought meals, and helped us during the past few years.

Eventually, I could see the handwriting on the wall. I was growing weaker and the looks on the faces of my doctors began to tell me that it was unlikely I was going to recover long term. When I looked into the faces of my children, I felt so sad. When I wasn't sad, I was angry. In my mind, if God loved me, he should help me get better.

But he didn't.

Eventually, after God tolerated all my yelling at him, the people close to us continued to pray and continued to love us. And I realized that even though God wasn't fixing my problem, that God was still loving me. He was loving me through all of you.

While I would not wish cancer on any one of you, there have been gifts along this road that I treasure. I was able to tell everyone close to me how much I love them. I was able to experience grace and love every day, even when I didn't really want it.

During one of the most difficult, but most important, conversations of my life, a special friend encouraged me to write letters. Many of you today have those letters in your hands. Please know that every page is anointed with my tears and my love.

> While I would change the story in a heartbeat so that Brad and the kids wouldn't have to go on without me, I feel closer to God and all of you because of what I have been through. I would have preferred to avoid suffering like this. But, God has been good to me, even in my suffering. For that, I am thankful.
>
> I love you all.
>
> Bethany

The only time you got choked up was when you read the phrase 'special friend'.

Bethany's story leads us into my next book, *How to Find Meaning in Your Life Before it Ends*. She's a great model to follow, and this new book provides two more great models as well as 101 ways to find meaning. She also makes a very touching appearance in the book I co-authored with my wife, Kristen Riecke. That book is called *No Matter How Small: Understanding Miscarriage and Stillbirth*, and is closer to our hearts than you can imagine.

PERSONAL REFLECTION

Part of my goal with this book is not only to help you figure out how to help other people in their time of crisis but to help you to look inside yourself a bit to see how these experiences affect you.

So, in closing, take the time to review some questions for reflection. If you need to pause after each question, reflect, or write some thoughts down, please take the time to do so. This might be the most important result of reading these stories.

How did you feel when Margaret prayed her 'angry prayer'?

Ed's death should not have happened the way it did. How did you feel when Ed's family kicked the doctor out? Could you see that this was headed towards a difficult conclusion?

How did you feel when you heard how Ed died? How could this have been avoided?

What did you feel the first time Bethany's dad called with her diagnosis? Try to name the emotion as specifically as possible.

How did you feel when you handed out the letters from Bethany and read the last one to the congregation?

THANK YOU

There are several great and practical help-sheets that I encourage you to read, but let me conclude with a simple thank you. Thank you for being willing to walk into Phase Three when so many people are not. The world needs more people like you. More people who will give Margaret their prayer requests even as her own go unanswered. More people who will hold on to Bethany's letters. More people who will push Ed's family to consider the end—before the end.

There is so much meaning and significance that is waiting to be mined, like gold, out of these painful stories.

It's hard work. It's quiet work.

It's important work.

So, thank you. If you have found this book helpful, would you please leave a review by clicking here or simply going to Amazon and search for "Patrick Riecke". Create a review today to help people like you find this important resource.

To help you further, consider these next steps:

- Read my book *How to Find Meaning in Your Life Before it Ends*
- Subscribe to our YouTube channel by searching for Patrick and Kristen Riecke
- Request your FREE Wallet Card to guide you on your next visit to a healthcare facility at PatrickRiecke.com/Resources
- Take my course on these topics and more, with lots of extra resources at PatrickRiecke.com/Courses
- Read *Giving a Life Meaning: How to Lead Funerals, Memorial Services, and Celebrations of Life*
- Book me to speak with your group for an hour, a day, or a weekend

ch. 12

No Matter How Small: Understanding Miscarriage and Stillbrith

Just a couple years after Kristen and I were married we had our first real brush with death as adults.

Young and in love, we decided it was time to start a family. In no time, we were expecting.

I was newly employed at a church that we loved. My income was very small, but we did have good insurance. And since, at the time, we planned to move overseas and do mission work, this seemed like perfect timing. We would have our first child stateside accompanied by some of the best medical care in the world. We would be surrounded by family and friends.

Baby Death

We announced the news of the pregnancy as soon as we possibly could to the joy of our parents and families. Ours would be the first grandchild on her side and about the 100th on my side.

A handful of months later we were at the doctor's office for an appointment when something happened for which I was unprepared. The tech was unable to find a heartbeat. I thought she just needed to look harder. I was confused.

By the time we left the office, I finally got the picture that Kristen understood immediately. Our baby had died.

+++

We named the baby Stephen.

We cried. And we cried and we cried.

I put my head on the shoulder of my pastor.

I yelled at God a few times.

I kicked the dog.

We collected items for the memory box.

Words of comfort were spoken by many.

And then, finally, I talked about it at church.

During a Sunday night prayer service, I shared what had happened and how I found comfort in remembering that God also lost a son.

Afterward, an elderly couple approached Kristen. Hank and Ginny Vernard. They were the sort of people that we all want to be when we are in our 80s. Sweet, loving, and kind.

Ginny's eyes were wet behind her bifocals when she held Kristen's hand and rubbed it.

The words she spoke next have never left us.

"It's been 50 years since we lost our baby. And he still holds a place in our thoughts and hearts."

There are no magic words to say at that moment.

Baby death, pregnancy loss, and infertility are topics I have left for a future offering. They deserve their own platform, but I didn't want to close this book without at least acknowledging this pain.

Kristen now leads multiple support groups for people who have encountered this pain in their lives in one form or another. The chaplains on my team respond every time a mother experiences this loss, whether her pregnancy had barely begun or the baby had a long stay in NICU.

Although the chaplains under my leadership do it far more often than I, I have many times held a baby in my arms who isn't breathing. It's one of the most sacred and painful things a person can do.

Here are five thoughts on supporting those who have experienced this pain:

- Treat the experience like a death regardless of gestation.

I have stood in hospital rooms with friends and patients after they have learned of the loss of a pregnancy or the death of a baby. The responses vary widely. Some moms, at least at the moment, seem untouched by what just happened. Others struggle to make it through that very first day.

But, you can't go wrong simply treating this as a loss. Treat her and the others affected like you would if anyone else in the family has died.

- They can use a funeral home.

Most people immediately think of the role of a funeral home when an adult dies. But in most places, funeral homes can be used for babies as well. Even if the mother was only a few weeks along into her pregnancy, she can elect to use a funeral home for services, burial, etc. Cremation is not usually a good option for ones so little but can be available in some circumstances.

Many years ago, when Stephen died, we did not know that we had the right to use a funeral home. Therefore, we didn't. We always wondered what happened to his remains. Now, working in the industry and being familiar with past practices, knowing what happened to his remains is a pain I can't change. It doesn't have to be that way anymore.

Using a funeral home isn't for everyone, but providing the option is important for everyone. Funerals can be expensive, but most funeral homes in the U.S. and many other places will find a way to reduce the cost greatly for baby funerals.

- Memory making is important.

As I shared, we have a "Stephen box" where we have a handful of items that help us remember our baby. If the baby is big enough, footprints and handprints can be done on special items. Pictures can be painful to consider, but a huge value later. Which family members come and see the baby at the hospital can be a tough decision. But generally, it is appropriate for the baby's siblings, step-siblings, grandparents, etc., to see the baby and hold the baby. In my experience, children handle seeing a dead baby much better than adults. At one baby's funeral, my small children walked straight up to the tiny casket and each one said, "He's so cute!"

Another special way to make memories is to wrap the baby in a family blanket, take pictures with a sibling's favorite stuffed animal or toy. Later, this will give you a frame of reference for the baby's size.

Any other activities you might do with a new baby who is born alive can usually be done with a baby who has died.

- Don't get tied up in controversial issues.

There are still, in many places, lots of political and religious controversies about babies, pregnancy, abortion, etc. Most people come into situations where someone has lost a child with some preconceived thoughts.

As a Christian pastor who grew up in the Roman Catholic Church, you can imagine that I have been exposed to a fair share of thoughts on when life begins, the morality of how we view babies and pregnancy, etc.

However, when I go into the room of a mother who is in pain, my theology only matters to me. As we discussed in chapter five, defending God or teaching theology at a time like this is generally a mistake unless you are the clergy leader for that person's faith community. Even then it is often unhelpful.

Never give a theological or political answer to an emotional question.

- Purposefully remember the baby.

Some people, after a few days or weeks, don't want to mention the baby to the mom, dad, or family, for fear of causing more pain. While this is a natural feeling, it's born out of our fears and pain, not the pain of those closest to the loss.

No mother of a baby who died, when a caring friend mentioned the baby, has ever responded, "Great, look what you made me do. You made me remember that I had a baby who died."

If they named the baby, remember the baby's name. If they used the name Abigail, ask about how they are doing since Abigail died. Be curious about their experience, within reason.

Did they get to hold her?

Did they take pictures?

Do they share the pictures?

If they share the pictures with you, they *will* be hard to look at. Just remember that this family not only had to look at pictures of a dead baby, but they also had to hold their dead baby in their arms.

If miscarriage or stillbirth has touched your lives or the lives of people you love, read *No Matter How Small: Understanding Miscarriage and Stillbirth,* a book my wife, Kristen, and I co-authored.

Each Christmas we hold a memorial service at the hospital for all those grieving baby losses. We talk about the babies. We share experiences. We light candles, and afterward, we have cookies and punch.

HOW TO TALK

At the very end of the service, I share an unusual benediction. Instead of speaking as the pastor, reading a prayer or scripture, or asking God to speak, I invite our deceased children to speak to us for the holiday.

Then I read the below to a chapel full of people who wish to God their babies were still with them, some of which would be five years old, others would be fifty years old, just like Ginny and Hank Vernard's baby.

> Perhaps our children would simply say, "I see you. And I know. I see that you love me. And I know that the separation between us causes you pain. I know better than anyone how much you love me. Although in your world, so much is cloudy, foggy, and confusing, I can see more clearly. And although I love you, my grief is not like yours. Your love for me is so palpable that I can feel it like a warm blanket wrapped around me. Your care and desire for me are like a blazing fire, both lighting my way and keeping me safe. What every child needs is to be loved. And you loved me and love me with all your heart. That is all I need from you. And you have given it to me. There is nothing more I want from you. What I want is simply your love.

And you have given that. I will not tell you not to grieve. But in your grief, know that I am perfectly cared for and perfectly loved. Although I know there are many things you wish you could tell me, there is only one thing I want to say to you. These two words capture everything I feel for you. The only thing I want to say to you tonight is this: Thank you.

Thank you for not forgetting me. Thank you for your expressions of love. Thank you for allowing my life to still impact you today. Thank you for allowing my death to soften your heart to others who mourn. Thank you for being my mom. Thank you for being my dad. Thank you for being my brother. Thank you for being my sister. Thank you for being my Grandma. Thank you for being my Grandpa. My aunt, my uncle. All I need is what you have given. Your heart and your love. So, allow me to leave you with these words: Thank you."

Help-Sheet #1: Healthcare Terms

Demystifying Healthcare: Some common terms

- **Brain Death**—Irreversible brain damage that has stopped independent respiration. In most places, Brain Death is considered the same as cardiac death. The time that brain death is declared will legally be considered the time of death.

- **Fetal Demise, Miscarriage, and Stillbirth**—Fetal demise, while a clinical phrase is the umbrella term used in healthcare to describe pregnancy loss at any stage. Usually, stillbirth describes a baby born dead later in pregnancy (after 20 weeks or so), while miscarriage describes pregnancy loss at an earlier stage. Moms of babies at any gestational age can have the remains of their baby released to a funeral home for burial services. Local statutes may apply.

- **Palliative Care**—Care for the alleviation of symptoms for the chronically or terminally ill. While no longer focused on 'curing' the person, the end of life is not necessarily soon. Palliative teams help a person to live the life they want while facing serious prognoses.

- **Hospice Care**—Care for patients when they are approaching the end of life. Still a high level of care, and the best for patients experiencing a slower decline and higher levels of pain.

- **Futile Care**—This strong term is only used when there truly is no hope of a positive outcome despite aggressive hospital care.

- **DNR**—"Do not resuscitate". In most places, only a physician can change this code status, in cooperation with the patient or the patient's surrogate decision-maker. A DNR does not mean the level of care should decrease, it simply means that if the patient loses his/her pulse, the care team will not administer CPR.

- **Advance Directives**—Your written instructions about your future medical care and treatment. By stating your healthcare choices in an advance directive, you help your family and physician understand your wishes about your medical care.

    - **Appointed Healthcare Representative**—A form that appoints a person to make healthcare-related decisions for a patient when the patient is unable to make decisions for themselves.

    - **Living Will**—A form that indicates patient preferences for end of life care

    - **POST forms**—Physician Order for Scope of Treatment. The POST form (sometimes called a POLST form—Physician Order for Life-Sustaining Treatment) is a standardized form containing orders by a treating physician based on a patient's preferences for end-of-life care. The form provides physician orders regarding CPR—code or no-code status; the level of medical intervention (comfort measures, limited additional interventions, or full intervention); use of antibiotics (for comfort only or full treatment); and use of medically administered nutrition.

Help-Sheet #2: HIPAA and Privacy

Privacy Basics for faith communities

- Ask your congregants to identify with your place of worship to the Healthcare Facility (Registration).
- If they have identified with your place of worship, you can call and get a list of your patients.
- If they have asked not to be in the public registry, staff cannot tell you they are at the facility. However, that does not mean you cannot visit. You will need to discover their location from family/friends.
- Do not share patient identification with others (name, room number, etc.).

- If you share patient information without the patient's permission, it is a violation of HIPAA law in the United States.

- Hospital staff may leave a voicemail at your place of worship about your patient ONLY if your voicemail box identifies your place of worship by name.

- Encourage your parishioners to let you know they are coming to the hospital beforehand when possible.

- Treat their information like news of a new pregnancy—let them tell their story—do not tell it for them. Many of the reasons for hospitalization are very private.

Help-Sheet #3: Patient Rights

Sometimes it seems you have few rights as a patient. However, it is imperative to understand that all patients with basic mental capacity have at least the following rights:

- Access to Care
- Quality of Care
- Privacy and Confidentiality
- Personal Safety
- Identity
- Information and Consent
- Communication
- Refusal of Treatment
- Transfer and Continuity of Care

- Hospital Charges
- Access to Medical Information
- Hospital Rules and Regulations

Help-Sheet #4: Medical Ethics FAQs

What are the guiding principles of medical ethics?

Beneficence—Is the proposed course in the patient's best interests?

Non-Maleficence—Will the proposed plan cause harm to the patient? First, do no harm.

Patient Autonomy—Has the patient indicated his/her wishes in advance? Respect for the self-determination of the patient.

Justice/Fairness—Are there legal questions or moral concerns that might affect decision-making?

Contextual Features—Are there concerns in the family or culture that have bearing on the care plan?

What might be an example of an ethics consult?
If a patient was unable to make their own decisions and there was a disagreement among qualifying family members about the course of treatment, that could be an ethics consult if there was at least some validity to each party's goals of care. Or, in a situation where a marginalized patient or voiceless patient needs support in decision making. Often critically ill patients for whom decision-makers are unclear can lead to an ethics consult.

What tools should be used to determine patient preferences?
Advance Directives can determine patient preferences. Other less official methods may not be binding but should be taken into consideration, including written notes and the spoken word as observed either by clinical staff or family of the patient.

Do patient preferences trump medical indications?
No. A patient request does not mean a physician needs to comply if the request is not medically indicated.

Who qualifies as a surrogate decision-maker?

The answer to this question varies from place to place. In the United States, this is a States Rights matter. That means, it can differ significantly from one state to the next. Additionally, it can change and be updated somewhat frequently. For example, in the State of Indiana in the USA, if there is no appointed healthcare representative or power of attorney for healthcare and the patient is not decisional, the following six classes may currently make healthcare decisions on behalf of the patient (but legislation is proposed for a change):

Spouse

Parent

Adult Child

Adult Sibling

Adult Grandchildren

Grandparents

Each member has equal authority and no consensus is required among the parties. Many states have a hierarchy–and Indiana's proposed legislation includes a hierarchy that is currently absent from the state code.

Help-Sheet #5: Tips for Hospital Visitation

I lead a team of hospital chaplains. Our patient census daily is well over 1,000 patients between all our hospitals. Our health system has over 2 million patient contacts per year and growing. Here are a few tips for visiting the hospital that we wish we could give to everyone.

For a really practical and free tool, visit my website for a wallet card containing things you should ALWAYS, SOMETIMES, and NEVER do when you visit a hospital. You can claim your free card at PatrickRiecke.com/Resources.

Privacy doesn't mean you can't visit—usually
Patient lists are available to your place of worship. Certainly, healthcare is shrouded in privacy. That's a

good thing, for the most part. But many people feel like that presents an insurmountable barrier between people in the hospital and the rest of the world.

That doesn't have to be true.

First, most health systems have a way for patients to declare a place of worship. Then, an official representative of the place of worship can get a list of everyone who is in the hospital who has associated themselves with that church/mosque/synagogue, etc.

Second, if the patient has allowed their name to be listed in the hospital registry it means that you can call the hospital, or stop in at registration, and ask about their location. It's simple. You just call and ask, "Can you give me the room number for Patrick Riecke?" If I haven't asked to have my presence kept private, and I am not a victim of violence or part of an ongoing police investigation, you will hear something like, "Yes, it looks like Patrick Riecke [they will probably mispronounce my last name] is in room 5116. Would you like me to transfer you to his room?"

But what if the patient is a private encounter (meaning they are not listed in the hospital registry), a victim of violence, or part of an investigation? Does that mean that you cannot come to see them at all?

Not necessarily. But the hospital will not be able to tell you where they are. If the patient herself contacts you and gives you her room number, you should be able to visit. One exception would be if she was a very recent victim of, or participant in, a suspected crime.

Utilize the social support staff at the hospital
Clinicians are always busy. Their specialty is medical care. But others in the healthcare organization have a bit of a different focus.

- **Chaplains** are there for the spiritual and relational needs of the patient and family. Chaplain presence and focus vary from one place to the next, but if you can connect with a chaplain, they can be a great liaison between the patient, family, and clinical staff.

- **Social workers** and case managers can help connect the patient with outside resources and help with discharge planning. In other words, they can answer the question, "what about when I go home?"

- **Patient advocates** are the first line of assistance when a patient is having a less than positive experience at a healthcare facility. They are trained to listen to the concern, log the concern, and ferret the story to the appropriate people around the facility to try to resolve the patient's concern.

- **Risk managers** often work closely with the patient advocates and the legal team of the hospital. Their job is to identify risk to patients, staff, and guests at a hospital or other facility. Once risks are identified, they also assist in finding an appropriate resolution. They can be a good resource when things are going awry with a patient and you feel the staff isn't doing their best.

Don't force prayer
Recently, I visited a family member in the hospital. Compared to many people in the hospital that day, his prognosis was good. As I walked in, the nurse was walking out to prepare his discharge paperwork. Despite his comparatively rosy situation, his disposition was anything but. He was grumpy and wasn't pleased with the nurse. I kidded him a little bit (like family members do) and then asked him if there was anything I could do for him.

"I guess you could pray," he said and held out his hands.

I smiled as I took his hand, put my arm around another family member, and started to pray.

He wasn't entirely sure he wanted to pray, and I don't blame him.

Think of it this way. Prayer is intimate. It's kind of like a polite kiss shared by a married couple. It's not the most passionate expression, but it's always somewhat tender.

A wonderful white-haired Catholic priest always wore a dark blue clerical shirt instead of the typical black. I worked with Father Ed Erpelding, a retired U.S. Navy Captain, for several years. He repeated to me regularly. "For many people, Patrick, a physical crisis is a spiritual crisis."

Crises are not solved simply and usually take time. Rushing a hurting person into prayer can be like asking a feuding married couple to kiss and make up—right now.

When you visit someone who is sick, it's ok to ask if they would like prayer. Here is how they might respond:

- They might say nothing at all. That means no. If they ignore the offer for prayer, it means they don't want you to pray right now, not that they never want you to pray for them.
- They might say something like "keep me in your prayers," or "put me on your prayer list". That means, I like the idea of you praying for me, but not right now. They might also be inviting you to leave instead of staying the extra few minutes to pray.
- They might say that they would like that very much and start to shift in their bed or chair. That means it's time to take their hand (once you have sanitized your own hands) and pray your heart out.

For more tools, videos on demands, and lots of free resources, enroll in my online course today at PatrickRiecke.com/Courses.

Acknowledgements

Thank you to Matt Burke and Tim Shapiro, with the Center for Congregations, for allowing me to lead the daylong workshops that gave birth to this book.

Thank you to Rev. Dr. Jon Swanson who not only gave input on those workshops but actually sat through my first time presenting. Then, he was gracious enough to wait 48 hours before giving me feedback. Jon also fielded a million questions from me about the writing process and the content of this book. Find Jon, among other places, at 300WordsADay.com. If you liked this book, check out Jon's book *Before You Walk In* and other titles in this series.

Thank you to Rev. Ann Steiner Lantz and Jeannine Nix for allowing me to see God at the hospital. And to Ben Miles, hospital president, for caring about the hearts and souls of his patients as much as their physical bodies and clinical care.

Thank you to Teresa Wedler and about three dozen other chaplains who have been such a joy to work with. Thank you for being the quiet presence of God during so many dark nights. You are heroes in my eyes.

Thank you to my parents who raised me to love God, people, and the mystery of faith.

Thank you, most of all, to my beautiful bride. Kristen, you are my heart. Most of what I have learned about caring for people has come from living with you. You are the most caring person to walk this planet since Jesus himself. When we were fresh out of college and I was in my first full-time ministry, we were serving a meal to the church and I called one of the parishioners by name. As they walked away, you looked over at me, smiled, and said, "I'm so proud of you."

"Why are you so proud of me?" I asked with a chuckle.

Acknowledgements

"You are learning people's names. That's so great," you said, in a totally not-patronizing way.

Thanks for your patience as I learn to be a better husband, father, and pastor.

More Grief Resources

Make an Impact on Your Group: Schedule a Live Presentation!

Have you enjoyed this book? Do you know of a group that would benefit from a presentation of this content? Go to PatrickRiecke.com and book Patrick Riecke to speak to your group today! Picture the concepts, education, and stories in this book, a life-changing conversation, and your group, better equipped than ever, to care for people in crisis. To schedule a keynote message, workshop or event go PatrickRiecke.com now.

E-Mail Newsletter

While you are on the website, for more free content, videos, and advice on helping people who are sick, dying, or grieving, sign up for Patrick's free newsletter! When you sign up, you will receive access to the five helpsheets in the back of this book, and several video trainings where Patrick explains how to do what we have talked about in this book. Visit PatrickRiecke.com now to sign up.

Purchase the Next Book in the Series

If you liked this book, purchase the next book in the series: *How to Find Meaning in Your Life Before it Ends.*

"Life does not mean something vague, but something very real and concrete." –Viktor Frankl

Would you like to find meaning in your suffering? Inside *101 Ways to Find Meaning in Suffering* you will gain concrete ways to discover meaning during your most difficult seasons. You will be inspired by compelling case studies. The dynamic list will help you find meaning in ways that are both profound and practical.

- 34 Words to Express
- 33 Actions to Take
- 34 Gifts to Provide

Miscarriage and Stillbirth

If your life has been affected by miscarriage or stillbirth, please read *No Matter How Small: Understanding Miscarriage and Stillbirth*. My wife and I co-authored this touching book that is both compassionate and honest. It is full of heart-rending stories and practical tools for understanding this personal topic.

Wallet Cards for Hospital Visits

You never know when you will end visiting a hospital. So, be prepared with a FREE wallet card telling you what to ALWAYS, SOMETIMES, and NEVER do when you visit a hospital. Claim your wallet card today at PatrickRiecke.com/Resources.

Online Video Course

Take your understanding to the next level by signing up for my online video course today. Not only will you have access to video teaching based on this book, but you'll also learn:

- How to select a funeral home
- How to talk with children about death
- The difference between pain medication

and assisted suicide

- How to perform advance care planning and find meaning in life

To begin my online video on demand course today, go to PatrickRiecke.com/courses.

About the Author

Rev. Patrick Riecke, M.A., is the Director of Chaplaincy and Volunteers and Chairperson for the Ethics Committee at Parkview Health. With over 20 years of ministry experience both in churches and in healthcare, Riecke is also an engaging speaker and is available for a small number of speaking engagements each year. He draws not only on his own experience but also on the daily ministry experience of other chaplains and friends. He holds a B.A. in Bible and Preaching from Johnson University and an M.A. in New Testament from Cincinnati Bible Seminary, with awards for scholarship and church ministry. Riecke lives in Fort Wayne, IN, with his wife, four children and enjoys having breakfast on his back deck overlooking their neighborhood pond.

For more content, social media links, to join his mailing list, or to book Patrick for an event, go to www.PatrickRiecke.com.

Made in the USA
Coppell, TX
25 February 2021